*God's* lent child

# God's lent child

*Women Who Found the Grace to Accept*
*What They Must Live Without*

## dejah fields

New York

*God's* lent child

*Women Who Found the Grace to Accept What They Must Live Without*

© 2016 Dejah Fields.

Published in New York, New York, by Morgan James Publishing. Morgan James and The Entrepreneurial Publisher are trademarks of Morgan James, LLC. www.MorganJamesPublishing.com

The Morgan James Speakers Group can bring authors to your live event. For more information or to book an event visit The Morgan James Speakers Group at www.TheMorganJamesSpeakersGroup.com.

## Shelfie

A **free** eBook edition is available with the purchase of this print book.

CLEARLY PRINT YOUR NAME ABOVE IN UPPER CASE

**Instructions to claim your free eBook edition:**
1. Download the Shelfie app for Android or iOS
2. Write your name in **UPPER CASE** above
3. Use the Shelfie app to submit a photo
4. Download your eBook to any device

ISBN 978-1-63047-730-1 paperback
ISBN 978-1-63047-731-8 eBook
Library of Congress Control Number:
2015912976

**Cover Design by:**
Rachel Lopez
www.r2cdesign.com

**Interior Design by:**
Bonnie Bushman
The Whole Caboodle Graphic Design

In an effort to support local communities and raise awareness and funds, Morgan James Publishing donates a percentage of all book sales for the life of each book to Habitat for Humanity Peninsula and Greater Williamsburg

Get involved today, visit
www.MorganJamesBuilds.com

Habitat
**for Humanity**®
Peninsula and
Greater Williamsburg
Building Partner

# dedication

This book is dedicated to the awe-inspiring women who labored in love to share their precious stories in this book. To help others, they gave the essence of their hearts.

# table of contents

Introduction     ix

Chapter 1     A Gift from God     1
*Dejah Fields*

Chapter 2     Our Reciprocal Agreement with God     19
*Dejah Fields*

Chapter 3     Someday . . . Forever     23
*Dejah Fields*

Chapter 4     Is Made Whole     29
*Pastor Riva Tims*

Chapter 5     The Memory of Danny Thompson     39
*Amber Carroll*

Chapter 6     Divine Planned Parenthood     51
*Lori Nichols*

Chapter 7     His Joy was My Strength     61
*Mary Greenfield*

Chapter 8     Slam Dunk for Jesus     71
*Dianne Timmons*

Chapter 9     Chad Sees....His Story     87
*Kasey Barerra*

Chapter 10     Afterword     99
*Dejah Fields*

# foreword

In "GOD'S LENT CHILD" Dejah has beautifully taken us on a journey by sharing how a mother embraces giving her dream back to God. Each mother's powerful story is unique to minister to any situation a mother may encounter. As you read each chapter, which is told from the heart of a loving mother, you travel through the joy and the pain of the time given to them with their child. They testify of the love of God and assure us that not only was He with them in their suffering, but He carried them through. Each mother sings a song of praise and celebrates a life with a grateful heart for the gift God lent them.

There is nothing more special than a mother's love for her child. As a mother of four children, I know the unbreakable bond that a mother holds for her children. Dejah shares how to relinquish our children into the heart and hands of God! This book brings healing, restoration, and understanding to mothers that walk in fear of their child dying; mothers that have gone through miscarriages, still births, and abortions. Dejah carefully removes the shame, guilt, rejection, and pain and brings understanding, peace, forgiveness, joy and strength. For, at the epicenter of this journey, we know that, "what the enemy counts as our destruction, God always turns around for our good!"

—**Riva Tims**
Pastor, Majestic Life Church
Orlando, Florida

## THE LENT CHILD

*"I'll lend you for a little time a child of Mine," He said,*
*"For you to love, the while she lives*
*and mourn for when she's dead.*
*It may be six or seven years, or twenty-two or three,*
*but will you, till I call her back, take care of her for Me?*
*She'll bring her charms to gladden you,*
*and should her stay be brief,*
*you'll have her lovely memories as solace for your grief.*
*I cannot promise she will stay, since all from earth return,*
*But there are lessons taught down there I want this child to learn.*
*I've looked the wide world over in My search for teachers true,*
*and from the throngs that crowd life's lanes I have selected you.*
*Now will you give her all your love, not think the labor vain,*
*nor hate Me when I come to take her back again?*
*I fancied that I heard them say; 'Dear Lord, Thy will be done.*
*For all the joy thy child shall bring the risk of grief we'll run.*
*We'll shelter her with tenderness; we'll love her while we may,*
*and for the happiness we've known, forever grateful stay.*
*But should the angels call her much sooner than we've planned,*
*We'll brave the bitter grief that comes, and try to understand.'"*

*Author unknown*

*Chapter 1*

# a gift from God

O h no," I screamed, "Mark, come quick, something's wrong with the baby!"

Frantic, my husband ran into the kitchen. His eyes grew wide with panic once he saw the floor.

He ran around shouting, "What should I do? What should I do?"

It all started on May 4, 1978, when we returned home from our first Lamaze class. I stood in my kitchen peeling potatoes. All of a sudden, I found myself standing in a puddle of water. This was my first baby. Never having any little brothers or sisters, I knew nothing of what to expect before giving birth. Something was wrong. My baby wasn't due for two months.

"Hurry, call the clinic," I shouted.

Mark grabbed the phone. When the doctor answered, Mark yelled, "There's water everywhere!"

The doctor instructed, "Get her to the hospital immediately."

We rode in scared silence to the hospital. Driving way above the speed limit, Mark tried to focus on the road. I tried to use some breathing techniques I learned earlier that day. My baby was due July fourth and, as the days grew closer, I could barely contain my excitement. I dreamt of my delivery day, but never like this. My bags weren't even packed and we had no guarantee that we'd make it to the hospital in time. All my excitement turned to fear.

The staff stood waiting for us, as we burst into the emergency room. A nurse wheeled me into a small room. Within moments, a doctor with a strong, determined face, azure eyes and coffee brown hair extended his hand, introducing himself as Dr. Berry. He began to examine me.

I kept thinking he reminded me of a doctor on General Hospital. By this time, my contractions were getting harder to breathe through.

Dr. Berry explained, "Your membrane has ruptured. Your baby will have to be delivered soon."

Fear gripped my heart, being only seven months into my pregnancy. After moving me into a larger room, they began a Pitocin drip to induce labor. They connected receptors onto my stomach to monitor my unborn child. It seemed like every time I had a contraction the baby's heart rate went down. Dr. Berry returned, explaining how they were trying to induce labor so I could deliver naturally, and that they were checking to see how much my cervix had dilated.

The nurses did their best to help me relax and breathe correctly during the contractions.

Chaos surrounded me. Nervous and scared, my whole body shook. Uncontrollable tears came with the fear of losing my first child. The frustration from the medical staff became apparent as their efforts to calm me failed.

Something was seriously wrong. Another doctor, with a mop of sandy brown hair and big, brown puppy dog eyes, arrived on the scene. He was Dr. Waczler, Chief of Staff. His demeanor was calm and confident, like a TV doctor.

"Unless you dilate more, we will have to remove the baby by Caesarean Section," he said.

I pleaded, "I don't want to deliver my baby that way, so please keep trying,"

"We'll give the Pitocin some more time to work," he continued.

For the next several hours, I was examined every fifteen minutes by both Dr. Berry and Dr. Waczler. They kept debating about how my baby would come into this world, and would come rushing in to give me oxygen each time the baby stopped breathing. Finally, they inserted a monitor, attaching it to the baby's head. This was a more accurate way of calculating the heart rate. All during this twelve-hour period everyone was kind and consoling. Not only was I exhausted from no sleep, I was also famished, since I'd had nothing to eat since the day before.

Another wave of panic washed over me when Dr. Berry and Dr. Waczler took my husband out of the room to speak in private. Seeing the concern etched on their faces, I could only guess at what they were talking about. Feeling left out of the whole ordeal, I demanded to know what was going on with my child.

Mark came over, took me by the hand and delivered the news I feared most. The baby's heart rate was dropping quickly. We had no choice but the Caesarian.

The medical team filed in announcing that, because this was major surgery, no one else was permitted to be in the operating room. I didn't realize they were worried that my baby might be stillborn and that I might hemorrhage.

As I entered the cold and sterile operating room, a sense of urgency and worry permeated the atmosphere. Alone, discouraged, and fatigued, I welcomed sedation. Metal objects passed in front of me and I could faintly make out faces. Everyone's words ran together in incoherent babble.

I awoke in excruciating pain with an intense thirst. It felt as though I had been sawed in half. I begged the nurse to give me some water.

She refused, saying, "It's too soon for you to drink anything. It's very important that you not vomit."

Not seeing my baby anywhere, I demanded to see my child.

The nurse evaded my questions. "The doctor will be in shortly to talk to you."

It seemed as though I lay there for hours in discomfort not knowing whether my baby had survived. Finally, a tall, tan man with blond hair and deep-set blue eyes came into my room. He introduced himself as Dr. Myles Grant.

"I am the Neonatologist taking care of your daughter," he declared with an Australian accent, looking like he just walked off the set of Crocodile Dundee.

Taking a moment to relish the thought of having a little girl, I prodded him about her.

Coming close to touch me on the shoulder he calmly explained, "You have given birth to a beautiful little girl weighing four pounds, one ounce, but she has complications from being born so early. She has severe jaundice, is on a heart monitor, her lungs are not fully developed and she could stop breathing at any time."

My heart pounded in my chest as I listened. I felt helpless.

Dr. Grant went on, "When babies are born so premature, the first forty-eight hours are the most critical. Please be patient. You will have to wait to see her. I understand how frustrated and scared you must be feeling, but please trust me. I'm doing everything I can for your daughter. We need to make sure she's stable before allowing anyone to see her."

Waiting the next two days was agonizing. The hospital staff was courteous, but they couldn't give me the one thing I wanted; my baby girl. The nurse brought regular updates about her, but my arms ached to hold my child. I will never understand why they denied me the right to see my own child. I guess the hospital staff thought that if I didn't see my baby, I wouldn't bond with her, and then, if she didn't survive, it would be easier for me. Didn't they realize I had already connected with the little girl I carried inside me for seven months, struggling alongside her to bring her into this world? Still, in so much pain and strongly medicated, it was hard for me to concentrate on what was happening. My reality became a nightmare.

After an eternity, a cheerful nurse named Rosie bounced into my room, almost singing, "It's time for you to meet your little girl. Please don't be alarmed by the harsh light over her. It's necessary to control the jaundice usually present in premature infants."

Gently, Rosie helped me into a wheelchair. I journeyed to the high-risk nursery, not knowing what to expect. Given a whole new vocabulary of medical terms regarding premature babies, I still had little understanding of them. I peered through the large window of the preemie nursery and saw many babies who didn't look sick; only small and helpless. My first impression was of how cheerful and colorful it looked. Unless you knew better, you would think you were in any normal maternity ward. It smelled like alcohol, diapers and baby powder. Painted on the walls were nursery rhyme scenes in bright colors. I remember thinking that the characters looked so real that at any moment they might come to life. I had never seen a cleaner place. Next to each individual icolet was a child's name and date of birth on a themed cutout, such as Raggedy Ann or Andy.

Searching the names, my eyes settled on one that said, "Malia". It seemed funny seeing her name printed out. Although this beautiful child was mine, I felt I didn't know her. She looked so tiny and helpless in that small, square, open box. A blindfold covered her eyes, protecting them from the strong light. A bow-type plastic cylinder around her head gave her oxygen. The light to control the jaundice was so strong, she was getting a tan. How funny it is that Caucasian babies are so white when first born, yet, here was my little girl, so brown. I kept thinking how she would fit right in when we eventually returned home to Hawaii. Around her wrists and ankles were bands with wires connected to a heart monitor.

Reaching out, longing to touch my precious child, I hesitated. Although I knew she was my daughter, the C section had made the birth so impersonal. A nurse took me into an operating room and hours later told me I had a baby. My desire was to deliver naturally; to see and feel my first child being born.

Rosie brought me into a small side room and helped me to scrub up. A moment later, she laid Malia in my arms. I froze.

A round and cheerful nurse with a big smile grabbed my hand and said to me, "Go ahead. You can touch her. Stimulation is good for her and you're allowed to take Malia out of the incubator and hold her one hour each day."

As my fingers gently stroked Malia's hand, a sensation of complete joy and love such as I had never known washed over me. Tears cascaded down my cheeks as I looked into the eyes of my miracle gift from God. That feeling, only a mother could know, has been with me since that first moment.

The nurses and doctors in the neonatal ward couldn't have been any kinder. They were always ready to answer any questions I had. Dr. Grant explained the mechanics of the surrounding machinery and stated that premature babies often require human touch and outside stimulation to start breathing again. This was the reason for the constant monitoring. Holding her ever so carefully, I told myself everything was going to be all right. Suddenly, an alarm sounded and a nurse ran over to Malia. The monitor alerted us that her heart had stopped. The nurses ran to her and began trying to stimulate her heart.

In shock, I screamed, "What's happening to my baby?"

The answer was one I had anticipated with fear. However, our journey was far from over. At the time, I had no idea that I'd have to endure this trial alone.

My husband, being young and immature, abandoned us a few short weeks after Malia's birth. He claimed he simply couldn't handle the pressure. Feeling helpless, like a little girl, I had no one to turn to. My parents had died five short years earlier. I was in a strange city with no friends. We had been visiting Mark's family, in Indiana, when I prematurely gave birth. Now I was stuck here. With my husband gone, his family proved to be of no help. The nurses and doctors of the neonatal ward became my support group along with the caring parents of other children who resided there. They were my family now.

Some days, after the sudden death of a premature child, I would visit the nursery only to see an empty incubator, and I would grieve for that lost child as if it were my own. One young family and I became very close. Their little boy, Zachary, was right next to Malia. He was the smallest baby in the high-risk nursery, weighing only one pound, four ounces. His family placed a themed cut out of a blue pickup truck on his incubator which led me to envision Zachary as a burly truck driver traveling down a country road. His parents and I encouraged one another. Zachary gained weight faster than Malia and he went home before her. It was a bittersweet day. I was happy for them but sad to lose their support and friendship. Zachary's parents promised to pray for Malia and to check on her.

About this time, a kind mother of six, who used her home for our Le Leche meetings, befriended me. Her name was Beth. With so many children, I knew I could learn everything about motherhood from her, so I gleaned from her knowledge. Confiding my fears to her, she spoke about how much Jesus loved me. But I was too angry and preoccupied with my own problems to listen. I couldn't understand how God could love me yet allow my daughter and me to face such hardships.

"Why would I want any part of a God that would do this to a child?" I asked Beth.

She replied, "He did not do this. He wants to heal her."

Beth went on to explain that God never changes. He is still in control, whether we're in the valley or on the mountaintop. She told me how God sent His only Son to earth to pay the ultimate price for my sins, that I could spend eternity with Him if only I accepted His free gift of salvation.

Beth recorded our names in her Bible and committed to pray for us daily. I believed her. I was struck by her kindness and the intensity of her love.

This left me feeling confused and uncertain about who I thought God was. On one hand, I was in a dire situation yet, on the other hand, I couldn't get over the thought that He loved me enough to sacrifice His own Son for me; and for Malia.

That night when I returned to the hospital, I decided to visit the chapel. Feeling awkward, I knelt in that small, dark chapel room. Words stuck in my throat but then began to flow, taking on a desperation I never knew existed within me.

Speaking to God like a long, lost friend I pleaded, "Please do not punish my daughter for what I've done. Please don't let her die. I'll give her back to You if You'll only let her live."

Immediately, peace overcame me. I knew I was in His presence.

"I thank You for sending Your Son Jesus to die on the cross in my place and I promise to raise Malia to love and serve You."

I walked away from the chapel with renewed strength.

At about the fifth week in the hospital, Malia's periods of apnea had ceased. Dr. Grant felt she was well enough to enjoy a full day with me without a heart monitor or the aid of the nurse.

Rosie escorted Malia and me into a large space set up like a hotel room. It contained a bathroom, sink, small kitchenette, and a couch. The walls were adorned with pictures of waterfalls and other beautiful scenes from God's creation. Although I was to be completely alone with Malia, Rosie handed me a small device with a button to press in case of an emergency. I spent the morning singing lullabies while gently rocking Malia in my arms. She was taking to nursing well and I felt that connection I longed for at her birth.

"Malia" I said, "when you're well we'll go back home to Hawaii and you'll play on the beach."

Just then, her head slumped backward and her lips turned blue. The life seemed to disappear from her little body. Holding my dying child, I froze.

At that moment, Rosie opened the door to check on us. She slammed down the button, and yelled, "We have an emergency. Hurry, get Dr. Grant!"

Within seconds, Dr. Grant and a team of nurses stormed into the room, taking Malia from me. Standing in stunned silence, my arms felt a chill where my darling daughter had rested her tiny head only moments before. Dr. Grant began to resuscitate Malia by inserting a tube down her throat and pounding on her chest.

Tears filled Rosie's eyes, and Dr. Grant turned around and punched the wall, hollering, "Come on; breathe!"

It was evident that not only had the staff become attached to my daughter, but they loved her and weren't going to lose her today if it was within their power. After a long pause, Malia began to sputter and gasp for air. The color returned to her cheeks and we all gave out a deep sigh of relief. However, it was obvious that she wouldn't be coming home any time soon. Malia returned to the Neonatal Intensive Care unit where she remained for the next five and one half months. Due to the relapse of her apnea, the doctors prescribed Phenobarbital, a powerful drug used to treat seizures. During one of the apnea episodes, she stared blankly and appeared unresponsive for periods of time. The Phenobarbital was supposed to make the apnea episodes less frequent and less severe and, ultimately, make them disappear altogether.

Returning to the small, temporary apartment I rented close to the hospital, I often felt as empty as the barren crib sitting there, but, during those times of solitude I was able to feel God's comfort. Yet, with each ring of the phone my heart would stop.

"Please God," I prayed, "let it not be bad news."

During the lonely days, I matured greatly. Beth stood by with encouraging words. I wondered about this woman. *She must have problems of her own,* I thought, *and, with six children, things must be difficult financially, but she always has a smile on her face.*

The day finally arrived when Malia could leave the hospital; the only home she knew outside my womb. Malia stayed on the same dosage of Phenobarbital but would eventually wean herself off of the medication. Dr. Grant warned me there was a possibility that Malia might have permanent brain damage or become blind due to the time she was deprived of oxygen. They said she'd have to be monitored to check both eyesight and development regularly. Due to her slow progress Malia received physical therapy at an infant development center each week. She visited her pediatrician, Dr. Arlene Meyers, bi-weekly to check her weight, eyesight, and lungs. Malia contracted severe asthma because of the resuscitation scar tissue and required a nebulizer to help her breathe. She spent the next year and a half in and out of the hospital due to attacks of asthma.

Having to be at Malia's side constantly, it was difficult for me to continue to work. Exhausted physically, emotionally, and financially I, once again, laid my child at the feet of Jesus. Realizing I could do nothing without Him, I attended a crusade event and stepped forward for prayer for Malia's healing.

Raising my hands, I prayed again, "I promise to give her back to You, just like Hannah did with Samuel."

The next day, when I arrived at the hospital, Dr. Meyers was waiting for me.

Looking bewildered, she blurted out, "This is astonishing. After checking your daughter's x-rays twice with the radiologist, I have no explanation for this. All the damage done to Malia's lungs, due to the constant need for resuscitation, is now gone. It looks like she has a brand new set of lungs!"

There was no explanation for it but, happily, I knew... *my daughter was God's miracle.* The God of the impossible healed her body of chronic asthma. He not only removed the scar tissue but gave her new lungs.

Since that time, so long ago, Malia has never had another episode of asthma. She never suffered blindness or brain damage. In fact, there have never been any long term effects from her premature birth.

In second grade, Malia shared her testimony at our church, Word of Life Christian Center, in Hawaii. Blessing the congregation, she sang "Rise and Be Healed." She graduated with honors and won countless ribbons while on the Kaneohe Swim Team. While in middle and high school, she traveled during the summers with Teen Mania Ministries' Global Expedition, to third world countries. She shared the gospel and the love of

Christ. One night, while she was ministering in Africa, God inspired me to write my own LENT CHILD poem:

### My Lent Child

*All my life I prayed to the Lord up above,*
*"Please give me a little girl I can love."*
*He answered my prayer,*
*"To you I have sent......*
*A precious child, for a time I have lent."*
*But she was born a little too soon,*
*She came in early May, instead of after June.*
*The doctors cried, "Oh no, she will not live,"*
*I prayed, "Lord save her, and I promise to give...*
*her back to You one day.*
*But now, I need her; please, let her stay."*
*The Lord answered my prayer,*
*"To you I have sent......*
*This precious child, for a time I have lent."*
*I prayed, "Thank you Lord, with Your Word*
*She'll be raised,*
*I'll teach her to know You, love You, and praise.*
*For her I'll stand in the gap, all of my days."*
*The Lord answered, "This day to you I have sent....*
*a precious child, for a time I have lent."*
*She grew in virtue, strength, and grace,*
*and in my heart held a special place.*
*She gave me her heart and love all the while,*
*and continually blessed me with her pretty smile.*
*Then one day, she said, "Don't be sad, I must go....*

*And tell the nations about the God that I know.*
*You taught me to pray, to listen, and yield;*
*Our Lord is calling me to His mission field."*
*I prayed, "Oh, Lord, it's true, you reap what you sow,*
*Now I'll honor the promise I made to You long ago."*
*The Lord answered, "A precious gift to you I have sent, but now*
*it's time to give back the child I have lent!"*

I am so blessed to have Malia (my *lent* child); my gift from God. I, continually, thank Him for her.

AFTERTHOUGHT: Since this miraculous experience, the Lord has graciously allowed Malia and me to return to St. Mary's Hospital in Evansville, Indiana where Malia spent five and a half months. With joy and gladness, I shared our testimony with those doctors and nurses who were not only a part of her life, but gave lovingly of themselves. While in town, I decided to visit a local church and you'll never guess who was in charge of the nursery when I went to sign Malia in. It was Beth!

Upon seeing Malia's name she started shouting, "Is this Malia and Dejah?"

I screamed in delight, "Yes, it's us!"

I ran up and gave her a big hug. She showed me, once again, in her Bible, where she had recorded our names and the date she started praying for my salvation and Malia's healing. God was so wonderful to orchestrate our meeting.

This experience not only strengthened me, but increased my faith and trust in God. I came to realize how much I needed Him and that I could do nothing without Him. Many times, since that time, He's given me the opportunity to share this testimony and pray with parents of children who need healing. When they come to the end of themselves, my desire is that they can find faith, hope, and strength in Jesus. All my life I wanted a little girl to love, and on May 5, 1978, my prayers were answered.

> Proverbs 3:5-6 (KJV) "*Trust in the Lord with all thine heart; and lean not unto thine own understanding. In all thy ways acknowledge Him, and He shall direct thy paths.*"

## Prayer

Dear Heavenly Father,

I come to You, today, to thank You for the child You have lent me. Looking at her, I know how much You truly must love me. She is so precious and exactly what I would have chosen for myself. This is a very trying time in my life but, when things get really difficult, that is when I feel You the closest to me. In the dark night of my soul when no one was there, as I cried until I didn't think there were any tears left, I felt Your love and Your presence. Help me to hold onto my hope and my faith. It is that faith and Your love that has transformed who I am and given me the strength to endure whatever may come my way.

The person I thought would be with me for a lifetime has walked away. He left when I needed him most. Jesus, I know Your friends walked away from You when You needed them, too. You became a man so You could feel the pain, loneliness, and rejection we feel. I thank You that, in Your love letter to me (the Bible), You remind me that You will never leave me or forsake me, but You will be with me forever. Help me to keep Your word in my heart and to always remember Psalm 121:1-2 (ESV) *"I lift my eyes to the hills. From where does my help come? My help comes from the Lord, Who made heaven and earth."*

I want to thank You for the dear people sent by You in that hospital to minister to my needs. They were family when no family was there. I pray for You to bless them and impart Your wisdom in them to help them care for those premature babies. To those who do not know You, bring the message of Your love and forgiveness to them. I especially lift up Beth, the woman who never gave up on me and relentlessly prayed that I would know You as my Savior and Lord. Bless her family and continue to use her to bring Your message to a dying world.

I thank You Lord that this isn't my permanent home. Someday, I will be in Heaven with You where there will be no more crying, pain, or death. Thank You for that blessed hope of an eternity with You.

In the name of Your Son, Jesus, Amen

*Chapter 2*

# our reciprocal agreement with God

*C*hildren are gifts from God He lends to us for a time. Some parents are allowed to hold on to theirs longer than others but, ultimately, they all belong to the Lord. Not only does God lend a child to us, but a child can also be *lent* back to God. We're given an extraordinary example of this in (1Samuel 1:4-20). In the story of Hannah, her husband, Elkanah, (in a culture of multiple wives) married both Hannah and Peninnah. Though he favored Hannah, she could not bear children. However, Peninnah bore Elkanah many sons and daughters. Back in that time, having a male child was considered a sign of God's favor and blessing. Barrenness left Hannah feeling unworthy and depressed, especially when Peninnah took every opportunity to rub it in.

After years of mistreatment, Hannah came to a place of great need. She went alone to the temple to cry out to God. Hannah's boldness could've been considered scandalous, since the custom of that day forbade women to go to the temple without their husbands. She offered a prayer demonstrating complete hope and trust in God.

Pouring out her heart, she prayed, "Oh, Lord of hosts, if only You will look on the misery of Your servant and remember me and not forget Your servant but will give Your servant a male child, then, I will set him before You as a Nazarite until the day of his death." Hannah determined that, if God would grant her the privilege of motherhood, she would gladly return her child to Him. God heard her plea. Out of great love, He gifted her with a child who she named Samuel.

To her honor, she kept her word. Hannah raised Samuel until he was weaned and brought him to the temple, as promised.

Filled with the kind of love only a parent could have, she said to Eli, the priest, "Oh my lord, as thy soul liveth, my lord, I am the woman that stood by thee here, praying unto the Lord. For this child I prayed; and the Lord hath given me my petition which I asked of Him. Therefore, also I have lent him to the Lord; as long as I liveth he shall be lent to the Lord." Hannah left Samuel with Eli to grow into a godly man. She gave her dream child back to God. Hannah visited Samuel every year, bringing a new coat she had made just for him. Hannah and her son Samuel pleased the Lord with their obedience and faith. Because of her trust, God continued to bless Hannah and allowed her to conceive three more sons and two daughters.

Sometimes, we hold on too tightly to the gifts the Lord has entrusted us with, whether they be possessions or people He's placed in our lives. We need to realize that, if we will allow Him, He will bless us so that our cup is overflowing.

Hannah was able to release Samuel back to God because she finally came to understand that our own children cannot be possessed or owned. We will never truly be happy if we define life by our possessions. People often remain depressed or bitter because they can't accept losses in their lives. We hold on too stubbornly to our fantasies and can't imagine our lives without them. Are you afraid of losing a child? Have you lost one and are still afraid to let that child go? Maybe, you even let a child go that should still be here.

To let go of this fear and pain, lose them (to God). Return that which you are most afraid to lose "back to Him". Hand everything that is precious to you over to God. There is safety in the hands of a loving Father.

The greater reason Hannah could give (return) her son back to God was the revelation that her real desire wasn't for a son, but for God Himself … to please Him and Him alone. Samuel was given to Hannah as if on loan for a time. Her act of devotion, in fulfilling her vow to God, was by returning to God what she had "borrowed" for a while. Samuel was a gift of God and consecrated to carry out God's purpose for His people. We can enjoy the gift God gives us, in the form of a child, knowing that His *most* precious gift, His love, will never have to be given back.

God, Himself, truly understands what it feels like when you have to let go of your own child. He gave all He had to us when He gave His one and only Son for us, as a sacrifice for our sins on Calvary.

*Chapter 3*

# someday . . . forever

*S*ome people live each day with guilt, pain, and confusion regarding the loss of a child through miscarriage, stillbirth, abortion, or early infant death. Jack Hayford wrote a book entitled, *I'll Hold You in Heaven* to bring hope and healing to those people through the truth in the Word of God. Jack Hayford is the founding pastor of Church On the Way, one of the largest churches in Van Nuys, California. So many people came to Pastor Jack with questions about these children that he decided to search the Bible for answers. The following are the questions and answers found in Pastor Hayford's book:

*Q:* "Was my unborn child, in the fullest sense of the meaning, actually a human being?"

*A:* Genesis 2:7 (KJV) *"And the Lord formed man out of the dust of the ground, and breathed into his nostrils the breath of life; and man became a living soul."* Not only has God given man the capacity to reproduce but, once life is conceived, that life must be honored.

Psalm 139:13 (NKJV) *"For You formed my inward parts, You covered me in my mother's womb."* This scripture shows us that God views life in the womb as real and eternal. The life in the womb is desirable and worth protecting. There is not only evidence of a real baby in the formation during the first trimester, but this human also has a lasting eternal soul that is present from conception.

In his book, Pastor Hayford wanted to recognize the permanent existence of the child that was lost through miscarriage, stillbirth, abortion, or infant death. He declares that those children still exist. Not only was each child a real, meaningful person, from the moment of conception, but each has continued to be a real, eternal being, since the moment of death. He goes on to say that your lost child is in God's presence and you will meet that child in eternity. You don't need to be worried or fearful of being accused by the child you aborted because Christ's death on the cross paid for all your sins and you are completely forgiven.

*Q:* "What is the eternal destiny of the unborn, stillborn, or early death child and to what degree does this life exist?'

*A:* Jeremiah1:5 (NKJV) declares, *"Before I formed you in the womb I knew you; before you were born, I sanctified you."* The life of our soul is an eternal spiritual continuum that begins at conception, continuing through and beyond birth. Our spirit exists from conception and beyond our eternal lifetime. When God said, *"Before I formed you I knew you,"* He was saying that none of us are an accident and that He pre-planned and provided for our life even while we were in the womb. When God said to Jeremiah, *"I ordained you as a prophet,"* He was saying that in every child there is not only the promise of God's purpose, but the provision of God's power to accomplish that purpose.

2 Corinthians 5:14-15 (NKJV)*"For the love of Christ compels us, because we judge thus: that if One died for all, then all died; and He died for all, that those who live should live no longer for themselves, but for Him which died for them and rose again."* Jesus died so that none of us would perish and He is a just God. Therefore, since these children are sinless upon death, they are immediately with Him.

Matthew 18:10 (NKJV) *"Take heed that ye despise not one of these little ones; for I say unto you, that in Heaven their angels do always behold the face of My Father which is in Heaven."* Their early departure, from life here, takes them immediately into God's presence.

When King David's son died, days after birth, he said, "I shall go to him." David was totally convinced he would be reunited with his child again in Heaven.

1 Corinthians 7:14 (NKJV) *"For the unbelieving husband is sanctified by the wife, and the unbelieving wife is sanctified by the husband; else were your child unclean; but now they are holy."*

This scripture confirms that, even if the parents were not believers, the children are innocent because they have made no moral choice.

*Q:* "How will you be able to recognize your child?"

*A:* 1 Corinthians 15:40 (ESV) *"Now there are heavenly bodies and there are earthly bodies, but the glory of the heavenly is of one kind, and the glory of the earthly is of another."* This scripture tells us that their heavenly bodies are identifiable.

In Don Piper's book, *90 Minutes In Heaven*, Don talks about his time in Heaven and says, "I knew what the Bible means by perfect love. It emanated from everyone I encountered in Heaven and I felt absorbed in their love. As I walked, I became aware of the wide variety of ages; old and young and every age in between. Every direction I looked, I saw someone I had loved and who had loved me. Over and over, I heard how overjoyed they were to see me and how excited they were to have me among them, but I knew they had been waiting and expecting me. Heaven is the greatest family reunion of all!"

While sharing about Heaven, Don testifies that he recognized people that he had known on earth. We too, can rejoice in knowing that our children who have gone before us will recognize and know us. They will run to us with open arms, full of love.

1 Corinthians 13:12 (ESV) *"For now we see in a mirror dimly, but then face to face. Now I know in part; then I shall know fully, even as I have been fully known."*

In Jesse Duplantis' book, *Heaven: Close Encounters of the God Kind,* he talks about when he was miraculously taken to Heaven. He states that he saw children carrying little harps; singing and praising God.

Jesse asked an angel, "Where did these children come from?"

The angel answered, "These are children that the earth did not want. God brought them here." He went on to tell Jesse that, "Children must be taught the oracles of God."

Jesse said he saw people and angels teaching the children. He then specifically asked, "Are you talking about abortions?"

The angel replied, "Yes, these children can't wait to see their mothers."

Hence, we know that there is no malice in Heaven and that these children have no ill feelings towards their parents who, for whatever reason, chose to abort them. They are awaiting the celebration when they will be reunited with their parents in Heaven.

Todd Burpo's book, *Heaven is For Real* (which is an account of his son Colton's journey to Heaven) also gives us information about children in Heaven. Chapter twenty-four of this book has Colton talking to his babysitter. She found Colton sitting up in his bed with tears streaming down his face. When she asked him what was wrong, he responded that he missed his sister.

When the babysitter offered to fetch his sister for him he said, "No, I miss my *other* sister!"

Colton had not known that his mother once had a miscarriage. The sister he missed was the one he had met in Heaven whom his mother had miscarried.

In chapter nineteen, Colton talks about the message Jesus told him to give to his parents. This message was that, "Jesus loves the children. They are precious to Him." Jesus even goes on to say that, unless we become like little children, we will not enter the kingdom of Heaven.

Matthew 18:3-5 (NIV) *"Truly I tell you, unless you change and become like little children, you will never enter the Kingdom of Heaven. Therefore, whoever takes the lowly position of this child is the greatest in the Kingdom of Heaven. And whoever welcomes one such child in My name welcomes Me."*

*Chapter 4*

# is made whole

*S*ometimes life does not turn out the way we planned. It is during those times that I am thankful that I have a loving God who is there every step of the way on the journey we call life. Not only is He with us when we go through difficult times, but He supplies the grace and strength to endure whatever situations we may go through. Our situation, however, may not change, but we do. With God's help, we can come through victorious.

A chill was in the air as I descended from the car on that dark, early October morning. As I walked into the hospital in Baltimore, Maryland, not at any time did I suspect that my life would change in a way I never expected. As they wheeled me down the hall to deliver my second child, I kept seeing OJ Simpson's face plastered on the TV monitors. I remember thinking that the entire country was following his trial. My doctor was not sure if I was full term. It was difficult for him to tell. I had given birth to my first child, Zoe, on Nov. 3, 1994. Three months after her birth, to my surprise, I was pregnant again. Then eleven months after having Zoe; on Oct 3, 1995, I gave birth to Zachary Tims 111.

During my pregnancy, everything seemed to be going well. However, in my last trimester, I began to bleed several times and went to the emergency room. Each time I was examined, my doctor assured me everything was fine.

He assured me, "It is normal. The blood is nothing to be alarmed about."

I felt devastated, but there wasn't anything I could do. He also advised me that nothing was detached.

When I went into true labor, my baby was born sunny side up which means when he came down the birth canal his head was faced up instead of down. The doctors endeavored to turn him as he came out. This took a while for them to do. I often wonder if that had anything to do with his later diagnosis. I didn't suspect anything was wrong because Zachary's Apgar scores were normal. His weight was somewhat low. He was only six pounds. I realized, at once, he was not progressing developmentally as well as his sister Zoe had. It was odd that I could see this at four months. I remember taking him to have baby pictures and, while watching the other babies, I realized something was not right. He wasn't able to sit up by himself or hold up his head.

My pediatrician advised, "Lets wait until he is six months old and evaluate him again". So we waited.

At six months, he was given a CAT scan and MRI which both showed that the mountainous regions of his brain, in many areas, were flat. The doctors diagnosed him with a severe type of cerebral palsy which affected his arms and his legs.

At one point, we considered suing the doctors in Baltimore because of what had transpired at his birth. The hospital staff just ignored us, and we didn't stand a chance against their high-priced attorneys.

At least in Maryland, we had the Kennedy Krieger Institute and John Hopkins. There was so much assistance available for Zachary that, in fact, some agencies even sought us out. Later, when we moved to Florida, we would have to learn how to search for programs and ask questions, although, I didn't even know what questions to ask.

As a child, Zachary couldn't feed himself or hold anything up. I had to do everything for him; even chew his food. Some children with trouble eating have to be given a G tube (Gastronomy tube) to make them receive enough fluids and calories to grow. The tube is inserted through the abdomen and delivers nutrition directly to the stomach. There are some risks and complications with this procedure. I was thankful when the doctors said it wouldn't be necessary for my son.

Zachary began attending the UCP (United Cerebral Palsy) of Central Florida. The UCP provides support, education, and therapy to children up to age 21. As a young mother, I had such a difficult time.

On Zachary's first day, I was sitting at a table with some other parents at the UCP, pregnant with my third child Zaria.

Then one of the workers there quietly said, "We need to talk". By her tone, I knew this wasn't good.

"Zachary is getting older and we need to discuss putting him in a wheelchair."

With that comment, I fell apart. I had never imagined my son in a wheelchair. My body began to shake and I couldn't hold back the tears of disappointment. Not one of the other parents comforted me. They looked at me as if I was crazy for never considering that Zachary might, one day, be in a wheelchair. They just didn't understand what I was feeling. Being pregnant, I was already flooded with a firestorm of emotions. Overwhelmed with wanting to do the right thing for my child, I began to sob uncontrollably.

I am a caregiver, so I don't often sleep throughout the night. I have a baby monitor in my room to listen for Zachary.

Sometimes his legs will get crossed and he may get wrapped up in the cover or need his blanket pulled up. He also may slide out of the bed and I'll have to put him back in and get him situated. He is unable to pull himself up. If he needs to go to the bathroom, I have to pick him up and put him on the toilet.

Throughout the years, Zachary has had a few surgeries to lengthen his heel cords and his hamstrings. He also had a minor surgery for his drooling. As he has gotten older, he is able to use his left hand. He is now able to feed himself and can eat solid food. He has a healthy appetite and eats more than anyone in our family.

As a result of his age, it has gotten increasingly more difficult because he is heavier now. I often reflect on the words of a song by the Hollies: *"But I am strong, strong enough to carry him, he ain't heavy; he's by brother."* This is how I look at Zachary... I never see him as a burden, although, I do get tired. I can see how caregivers, if not tempered by the Holy Spirit, can turn angry on their patients. It takes patience and the grace of God to care for someone who is completely and totally dependent on you; to clothe them, feed them, bathe them, and transport them places. This requires total dependence on the strength of God.

When I look at my son, and feel depleted, I see him through the filter that God must look at us. Just as Zach is helpless in many ways, we often find ourselves helpless before the Lord. Where would we be if it were not for the Lord on our side? In Galatians 6:2 (KJV) we are commanded to: *"Bear one another's burdens and so fulfill the law of Christ."* The law of Christ is love. The ultimate example of bearing one another's burdens is shown by the sacrifice of Jesus on Calvary. He took our place so we could have redemption for our sins and eternal life.

Zachary is not able to walk and is still in a wheelchair. However, at this time, I deal with where he is (for now), by faith. I hold onto the Word of God and believe someday he will be completely healed.

As for me, I look at my son Zachary as the joy of my life. He is a faith builder. He is always a happy, joyful child who is singing all the time. He is not an avid reader and does not do well academically, although he is very adept with technology. It is amazing to watch him maneuver through programs on his iPad and computer despite the fact that he is unable to read well. One time, he found himself in a program that was in Chinese and he was able to navigate as if he knew what was going on. God has truly gifted him in that area.

Now that he is eighteen, he has the same desires of any teenager. He wants a girlfriend, a job, to be able to drive a car, and to have a marriage someday. He looks questionably at me and, as he watches his eleven month older sister, who is in college, he wants to do what she does.

He asks me, "When can I do these things?" At times, it has gotten difficult to deal with this aspect; now that he's thinking about these things. This is an area I am taking before the Lord, and I know He will give us the grace to deal with it.

Zach has three siblings (Zoe nineteen), (Zion fourteen), and (Zahria fifteen). They love him dearly and, like any family, they play, argue and tease one another. Zachary makes up for his lack of mobility with a biting wit.

I say to them, "Why don't you walk away?" It is pretty hilarious to watch them just stand there and take whatever Zachary inflicts. My children hold him to the same standards they set for each other. They sometimes have a hard time believing anything is wrong with their brother.

Late at night, after putting Zachary to bed, I hear him worshipping God. I realize that my son has a childlike innocence and trust which has not been tarnished by the things of this world. In the scripture Matthew 18:3 (NIV), "*Truly I tell you, unless you change and become like little children, you will never enter the Kingdom of Heaven,*" Christ points to little children as the model with which members of God's kingdom must emulate themselves. The attributes of children are humility, trust, blissful dependency, and teachableness. The direct opposite of these attributes are distrust, self-focus, a critical nature, and worldliness.

It's sad how, as adults in this world system, we have learned to question and distrust. As I listen to Zachary singing one of his favorite songs, "I Worship You," with such love and faith, I realize this is how our God wants us to approach Him. Zachary also loves to sing in our church, performing solos of his favorite songs, "Praise Is what I Do" and "Let It Rain". He totally understands worshipping God.

As a single mother of four children, pastor of a large church and the sole caregiver of an eighteen year old boy with cerebral palsy can be exhausting. I have supportive parents and a wonderful congregation but, late at night, when I am lifting Zach in bed or taking him to the bathroom, I think about how many times my Heavenly Father lifts me up and holds me.

Serving my son gives me a deeper love for my daddy God who takes care of all my needs. It gives me a better comprehension of the dynamics of unconditional, agape love. I realize how much more I can give to my own flesh and blood. This type of love is not based on what my son can do for me, but instead on what I can do for him.

I consider it a privilege to love my son and be entrusted to care for him. I tell other parents with special needs children that not only is their child special, but they (the parents) are special as well. God designs families. He chooses the perfect parents for a specific child. There is something in you that God saw as fit to be able to love and care for this child. He places you on the positive end everyday as He unfolds his plan for their life. Instead of looking at your circumstances as traumatic or stressful, look to see how God will get the glory out of it. Always, remember that your child has a purpose in God's kingdom. Whether or not he is healed while on this earth, we have the assurance that he will be whole and healed in Heaven. Children have a call on their lives which is encompassed with the challenges set before them. Likewise, you have a call on your life dealing with these challenges alongside them.

Two scriptures that I have leaned on are Romans 8:28 (ESV) "*And we know that for those who love God all things work together for good, for those who are called according to His purpose,*" and Proverbs 3:5-6 (ESV) "*Trust in the Lord with all your heart, and do not lean on your own understanding. In all your ways acknowledge Him, and He will make straight your paths.*"

I know God has a plan and a purpose in all that happens to us and I trust Him. He always equips us with what we need. We have to trust the Lord through it all. With His help we will get through it. Our Heavenly Father will help us get over the grief we encounter. He guides us to make the right decisions that will be best for our children. When all our strength is gone, He lifts us up and renews our spirit.

Being a mother of a special needs child has propelled me to my destiny. Not only has it given me a more tender heart to connect to people in a deeper way, but it has allowed me to be able to relate to their pain. It has truly been an honor and a blessing to be Zach's mother. I know God gave me the perfect child and Zach has the perfect mother for him. I believe that there is a call on his life for healing. What he's going through God will use to help others. I believe that God is going to heal my son and I stand on God's Word for his total healing.

## Prayer

Dear Heavenly Father,

I thank You, today, according to Isaiah 40:31, that, if I hope in You, then, You will renew my strength like an eagle... *I will run and not grow weary; walk and not faint.* Being a caregiver for my son can be demanding but it's Your supernatural strength that gives me the faith and hope to keep walking the path You have ordained for me. May I always stay close to You with a heart willing to listen, my loving Father.

My precious son is a miraculous gift sent from You. I daily, expectantly, await Your wisdom to preserve the son You have entrusted into my hands. I am so grateful that You picked me to be his mother. I pray for constant aid from the Holy Spirit that I might have the words to speak to Zachary to encourage holiness. I pray for the patience to give guidance and discipline, as led by You, and the knowledge to know what my child needs and how to respond to his many questions. Let me be the best mother I can be so that I can help my son grow in his love and faith in You; while bringing others to Jesus. May I constantly remind myself that this child belongs to You, ultimately, and is simply on loan to me.

I ask all this in the name of Jesus.

# the memory of danny thompson

*I*t is hard to imagine that Tanya and I embarked on this incredible journey a mere nine years ago. As I look around this elegant ballroom, I see so many of the faces I have grown to love over these many difficult and trying years. While I prepare to ascend the steps of the stage to accept the *Excellence in Clinical Research Award,* I cannot help but reflect on my past and the specific events in my life that have ushered me toward such an accomplishment. Looking at my beautiful wife Tanya who has given nothing but support, I realize I could not have hoped for a more devoted and loving partner.

My mind drifts back to our second year in college where we both studied medicine at UCLA. I was outgoing and headstrong while she was soft spoken, tenderhearted, and had a real love for God. We were quite the odd couple but I was determined to make it work and knew right away I could deny her nothing.

We dated for three months before I finally persuaded her to take our relationship further. Tanya was uneasy at first but, with a little more pressure, she eventually gave in. After all, we loved each other and wanted to spend the rest of our lives together and this seemed like the next step. We always played it safe, so my shock was quite evident when she shared her life-altering news one night over dinner. I wasn't ready to be a father, just then, nor did I think I would ever be.

"We're still young…What about our dreams, Tanya? Have you considered what having a child right now would do to the plans we've made? There is too much at stake to even start contemplating a family this soon," I pleaded.

I could tell that I had hurt her, but what she wanted was impossible. Was she really willing to throw away her dreams so she could raise a child? I planned to stand my ground but was completely unprepared for her next words.

"But Danny, it is already done. You're a father now, even if our child has yet to be born," she reasoned with me. I gave a loud sigh. She had me there. How could I possibly argue with that logic and yet keep our relationship alive?

"We can always look into adoption. The baby will have a good home with loving parents who are both emotionally and financially ready for that type of commitment," I countered quickly.

Looking resolute in her decision she said, "We can still live out our dreams while raising this child and I will do whatever it takes to make that happen. I will take time off from school and work part-time until you graduate and complete your residency. Don't you realize that this child was a gift from God meant just for us?"

In my heart, I knew she had won the argument. Though she had talked me out of adoption, I still felt uneasy about raising a child. Flashbacks from my early childhood reminded me of the beatings I'd been forced to witness my mother endure at the hands of my drunken father. Not only did she shield me from his attacks but, when he was gone, she would gather me in her arms, rocking me while sobbing softly.

Whispering in an almost pleading way she'd say, "It's okay, Danny. Mommy loves you and will keep you safe. I will protect you."

I would lie against her, my head resting on her chest as her heart thudded in a strong steady rhythm. It was just her and me in the world and nothing else mattered. What if I could not give that kind of selfless love to this child… or worse, would become like the man I once feared?

I still had my doubts until our nineteenth week check-up. The excitement finally began to affect me as I realized perhaps we were making the right decision, after all. Seeing my little baby on the monitor sealed the deal. I knew I would do anything for this child.

"I hope you like the color pink because you'll be seeing a lot of it: you're having a girl!", the radiologist happily announced.

Thoughts of a future filled with baby dolls and daddy-daughter dances began to play through my mind. Tanya and I held hands, lost in our own thoughts, imagining our new lives as a trio, when we suddenly realized the radiologist had grown very quiet.

"Is everything okay?" Tanya asked.

"I'm not at liberty to say, but the doctor will go over the results of the exam when he sees you," she said.

I felt Tanya tense up.

With heavy hearts, hand in hand, we walked slowly into his cold, sterile office preparing ourselves for the news to come. We waited anxiously for our obstetrician to come into the exam room and tell us everything looked great, but that would have been a lie.

"The sonogram has revealed an abnormality in the fetus' lung development. I suspect that cystic fibrosis is the prognosis but I cannot be certain until the results of the blood work come back. I must tell you, however, I've seen symptoms like this before and it doesn't look promising. Fortunately, you are not too far into this pregnancy and can choose to terminate it and try again within a few months."

"How can you even suggest ending my pregnancy?" Tanya asked with trembling lips, "My child is alive... Come feel her kick as she moves around!"

"I am not trying to be cruel". The doctor continued, "I just want you to understand that, if I am correct about this, you can expect a future filled with frequent medications, breathing treatments, and hospitalizations just to keep her alive. That is no life for a child."

I gripped the armrest of my chair because the room felt as if it were spinning. I once feared I might not be able to protect my child but now it seemed even her own body was attacking her. Tanya, however, was steadfast in her decision that our baby deserved a chance at life and only God would have the final say.

We began seeing a specialist for the prenatal care of our daughter. It was during this crisis I began to attend church for the first time in my life hoping to find comfort. Temple Baptist Church became our home, as Pastor Carlos quickly made Tanya and me feel like part of the family. As I poured myself into the Word of God, I felt God's desire for a relationship with me. Two months before the birth of my daughter, I surrendered my life over to the Lord. At that moment, peace descended on me as I realized God was in full control of my child's life and that He loved her more than I ever could. Regardless of the outcome, I knew everything was going to be okay.

Tanya and I joined our church and set a date to get married that fall. From there on out, we were going to live our lives God's way.

Jennifer Nevaeh Thompson was born two days before her due date weighing a healthy seven pounds, six ounces. Her hair was jet black and thick with curls; her lips plump and rosy. The doctors were quick to rush her away to the NICU, right after her birth, until she could stabilize and breathe on her own. After many long weeks, we were finally able to bring her home.

Jennifer was a perfect baby in that she wasn't very fussy, slept through the night, and ate very well. She was our beloved miracle child and we treasured every moment with her as if it were the last. Her lungs, not opening fully, sounded wet and raspy as she took each breath. It was hard to see my little angel attached to a nebulizer everyday knowing that she would be dependent on several medications for the rest of her life.

It was due to this frustration that I joined a medical research team in search of a cure to end this debilitating disease and ease the lives of those afflicted with it. Beginning my study, I was greatly saddened to discover that eighty percent of families faced with the reality of cystic fibrosis and other challenging medical problems choose to terminate their pregnancies. I found myself struggling with the knowledge that many medical professionals felt this decision was in the best interest of the family and actually encouraged them in making it. How wrong they were, and children were paying for it with their lives! With this realization, I vowed to stop at nothing until a cure was found.

I clearly remember my dear Jennifer's fifth birthday as if it were only yesterday. We joyously celebrated a life that had flourished five years longer than doctors believed possible. Everyday was a challenge as she constantly relied on multiple medications to help her lungs function properly and she could not physically exert herself very much. Our weekly schedule consisted of trips to the doctor's office, pharmacy, and physical therapy. Though Jennifer's life seemed harder than most children, she was always filled with such love and enjoyed each day to the fullest. I could never imagine a world without her in it.

It was during this time we made serious progress with our research by isolating and repairing the mutated CFTR gene. Jennifer was among the first treated in clinical studies at age eight and her symptoms quickly began to subside. Though the medical community treated this as a gold mine, my family knew this miracle for what it truly was; an answer to our prayers.

Jennifer's brush with destiny has been a turning point for her. As if in mockery to the doctors who wished to deny her life, she has begun to swim, run and play games like other children her age. Having seen a real need of love and compassion for children suffering from disabilities, she began to befriend and mentor those in need. Just last week, she read me an essay she wrote for school. In it, she said she was going to be a doctor, just like her daddy, when she grew up. I couldn't be more proud of my little girl.

With that last thought, a bone-chilling shiver pulled Danny back into the banquet hall. It was time to give his speech. As

Danny Thompson stood up from his seat and approached the podium, a strange feeling began to creep over him. Looking to his family to see if they too had noticed the change in atmosphere, his eyes rested upon his daughter. Never looking away from her father, Jennifer simply vanished from her chair as if she never existed. Startled and frightened, he turned to Tanya in hopes she could make sense of what had just occurred but, as he did so, she, along with everyone else in the room, began to flicker and fade from sight. Darkness consumed the room almost immediately and the tables appeared overturned and unused.

Danny cried out as he stood completely alone and lost in this abandoned hall when suddenly a woman's sobs intruded upon the foreboding silence. Her words hauntingly echoed her misery throughout the room. Danny held his breath so that he could make out the meaning in her words.

"Mommy loves you and I wanted to keep you safe,"

His knees began to buckle as he heard the last words come out in a choked cry,

"I am so sorry Danny! Why didn't I protect you?"

And with that sudden revelation, Danny's life story ceased to be.

Danny Thompson's mother had succumbed to the pressure of her boyfriend and the doctors and made the choice to abort her child. Everything that Danny was and would have accomplished could never be. Along with the loss of a great man who would have benefited society, beautiful Jennifer was never allowed the chance to come into being.

Just how many lives does one abortion affect?

Psalm 139:13-16 (ESV) *"For You formed my inward parts; You knitted me together in my mother's womb. I praise You, for I am fearfully and wonderful made. Wonderful are Your works; my soul knows it very well. My frame was not hidden from You, when I was being made in secret, intricately woven in the depths of the earth. Your eyes saw my unformed substance; in Your book were written, every one of them, the days that were formed for me, when as yet there was none of them."*

***Sidenote from Dejah Fields:*** The fictional Danny of this story represents all of the aborted children who were never given the opportunity to express their creativity or contribute something to this world. But, as was presented in Chapter 3 and as Jack Hayford argued, the (inspired of God) Bible clearly takes the stance that God holds these children, safe in his arms.

January 22, 1973, is a date that will never be forgotten in the United States. It was on this day that the Supreme Court handed down two infamous decisions: Roe Vs. Wade and Doe Vs. Bolton. As a result of what has followed, as is stated in the 1983 Senate Judiciary Committee Report, "No significant barriers of any kind whatsoever exist today in the United States for a woman to obtain an abortion for any reason during any stage of pregnancy." Since the legalization of abortion in 1973, there has been approximately 50 million abortions performed in the United States alone.

I remember back in the early 1970s, when I escorted a close friend of mine to Planned Parenthood, to see if she was pregnant. When they told her the test was positive, they casually mentioned abortion as the best option. Of course, they told her a baby, at his time, would just complicate her life. She would have to drop out of college and probably go on some government assistance program, not to mention that she would probably lose her boyfriend because he was not ready to be a father or mature enough to handle any type of commitment. They never referred to the baby growing inside of her as a "child". She was just told it was a "lump of tissue". At that time, there were no pictures in the typical doctors' office of the developmental cycle of the fetus and no ultrasounds given.

My friend went along with the *procedure*, as they called it. Unfortunately, it did mess up her life. She carried guilt and shame with her for many years. It was so bad that, if someone was wheeling a baby in a stroller, she would have to walk across to the other side of the street. One time, I was in a dentist office with her and someone came in with a new baby. And my friend went running out the door.

When she, eventually, got married and tried to have a child, it was difficult for her to carry a child full term due to the internal trauma caused by the abortion.

It wasn't until someone gave her a copy of Jack Hayford's book "I'll Hold You In Heaven" that she was able to receive the forgiveness for what she had done, as she gave her heart to Jesus.

The sad part is that women seeking abortion and an easy way to fix their problems are usually never told the truth. Abortion is a major surgical procedure and is not safer than childbirth. It has been medically proven that, after an abortion, a woman faces increased possibilities of future miscarriages, tubal pregnancies, premature births, sterility, and long lasting emotional trauma.

I often wonder, when I see the statistics of the staggering number of abortions performed daily, if one of the children murdered could have changed history. Could one of them have been another Abraham Lincoln, Mother Teresa, or Jonas Salk? Maybe one of these children might have been the researcher who discovered and developed a cure for the deadly disease of cancer.

In Jeremiah 1:4-5 (ESV) *"Now the Word of the Lord came to me, saying, Before I formed you in the womb I knew you, and before you were born I consecrated you; I appointed you a prophet to the nations'"* God knew, sanctified, and ordained Jeremiah to be a prophet while still in his mother's womb. God already had a purpose and a plan for this child to be a great prophet.

I am thankful for the technology, research, and crisis pregnancy centers available today, but we need to witness to the sanctity of life and pray for our nation. In the Old Testament, the prophet Jeremiah proclaims:*"A voice is heard at Ramah, lamentation and bitter weeping. Rachel is weeping for her children; she refuses to be comforted for her children, because they are no more."* Jeremiah 31:15 (ESV)

## *Letter From God*

**My Child,**

   **Now that you have given your heart to Me, I want you to know that I forgive you for having an abortion. When you came to Me with true repentance, I remembered your sins no more. When I died on the cross for you, your sins were washed**

*away by My blood. Stop beating yourself up with guilt. When I said the words, "It Is Finished" on the cross, the debt for your sins was paid in full. Receive My forgiveness, joy and peace. Use what you've been through to help others not make the same mistakes. I want you to know that your precious child is here with Me, in Heaven, awaiting your arrival, someday. We both love you.*

*Your Heavenly Father*

## Chapter 6

# divine planned
# parenthood

A t age 32, I had been like a mother to so many other children, being the oldest daughter in a family of ten kids. I always loved and wanted children of my own, but I sensed that I needed a miracle. Any doubt that the Lord would intervene lifted one day while I was on the 700 Club telephone prayer line when I called during a bout of loneliness - having just moved across an ocean to a new home in Idaho.

The man on the other end of the line was a pastor who suddenly got a case of the giggles. I had experienced this sensation before, where an otherwise somber and serious moment could erupt into lighthearted banter due to the overshadowing presence of the Holy Spirit. This was a good sign that the Lord was, at that instance, communicating something in the Spirit, and I knew to listen intently. The man asked if I was hoping to have a baby and, before I could give the answer, he proceeded to tell me, in a celebratory fashion, to get ready because a baby was coming my way.

Sure enough, it was within a week that I heard the words over that same phone line but now connected between me to Wisconsin with a woman who was single, a mother, pregnant, and overwhelmed, "Would you like to adopt this baby?" I followed through to receive this child that the Lord had, obviously, picked out specifically for me and my husband. I was there for the delivery and my parents rode with us back to Idaho for the baby's journey to his new home. We named him, "Evan," which means, "gift of God" as it is a Celtic name for "John". He was always an adorable child and, although strong in temperament, I always knew he was truly a gift to us. I continue to expect that there are still great things ahead for him with the Lord going before him to lead him.

Though, I would have been satisfied with one child, one day three years later, I began to suspect the Lord was not finished. I told my husband that I had experienced a kind of vision and that I somehow knew that the little blond toddler in the picture was my own child, yet unborn. In this vision, the child was standing in my brother's farmhouse in Wisconsin.

Some time later, I was attending a retreat with my mother and three sisters. In the middle of the most intimate ladies' meeting of the week-end, the woman next to me interrupted the meeting to tell me that I was going to have a baby. She whispered in my ear that it would not be easy and I would suffer with the pregnancy. That part of the woman's message also came to pass and I did have an extremely difficult pregnancy. That journey, and the strength the Lord provided every step of the way, is a story unto itself. I do not remember myself being burdened during those struggles but only filled with joy. The woman added one other detail. She felt the child was to be named "Nathaniel" which, by the way, means "gift of God".

It was an hour before going to the hospital for the eventual delivery of this child. Though my husband had not been pressed by me to name the child Nathaniel, after he had lain on the couch for half an hour, determined for a name for this child, he jumped up, smiled, and exclaimed, "His name is, Trevor Ethan Nathaniel Nichols".

Guess what? I was already pregnant, but didn't realize it, when this woman delivered this news to me. A few days later, I had an odd craving for strawberries. I remember asking my mother (remember she was the mother of ten) what the symptoms of pregnancy are. I got irritated when she would not stay on the subject and she later admitted that she had no expectation that I would ever get pregnant. So, with a bit of an attitude, as soon as I got home from our trip to the library, where she had evaded my questions, I marched down to the grocers and picked up a pregnancy test strip and a carton of strawberries. I remember those moments, as if it was yesterday, of sharing the strawberries on the floor of my parent's guest room with my son and reading the positive test strip. My shocked and surprised mother got to hear the news even before my husband, who was traveling, but I just had to enlighten her that the Lord can open any womb.

We were living in sunny Oregon when the baby was born. By the time he was one year old, we were, by then, in a transition again and staying for a few weeks at my brother's farm. It was interesting to watch this little blond boy toddle around underfoot in the very surroundings of the earlier vision I had, playing with his cousins.

But wait! — as the loud announcers in the TV product pitches for commercials would shout to express this very vital aspect of my saga — apparently, the Lord wanted to make it clear to me, or perhaps to you and those I tell this story to, that He is the one who opens wombs and He is the one who closes them. You see, I had been more than elated to have my adopted gift (my first son) and, then, my second son, through a seemingly miraculous birth, so you imagine my joy when, on my fortieth birthday, I had a positive pregnancy test.

Maybe, I need to tell you something a bit more amazing to help you see what made it special. I had gotten an actual video-taping and description of my female insides by a specialist/obstetrician during a minor surgery procedure. Afterward, he came to my outpatient bedside (NOT routine) to tell me that I had no functioning hardware. He said my tubes (that deliver eggs) were obliterated and the ovaries were not recognizable and could not possibly do proper work to make babies and that the conception was only part of the problem as carrying a baby would not be feasible either. I was touched that he cared about a forty year old so much but assured him that I had gotten pregnant with this equipment once and that I could again.

He looked over at my son, sitting nearby, and said, "Well, that's a God-thing, then."

And he was right to say so... Three months later, he was taking an ultra-sound of my living embryo with beating heart and all. Now, he was using phrases like, "I need to put this in a medical journal!" This otherwise low-key, mild-mannered physician became quite animated. It was as if his personality had changed completely.

You can imagine how strange that all seemed to me when I started to miscarry Easter Sunday of that year. When I did finally come in to do the procedures of a miscarriage, my fears that I had let the Lord down, by not holding onto this miracle full term, were alleviated.

At the office, as I saw the tiny figure be delivered, even in its weakened state, I was in awe of God's awesome creation that I was witnessing. I had asked the doctor to save the baby's body in preserving fluids for me. He was impressed that I wanted to treat my baby with respect and have a burial. Then, he said something that made the whole loss easier for me.

He said, "We doctors think we know so much, but we know nothing. These God things are amazing! I have been fooled once. I believe that you could come back pregnant and fool me again."

God's plans often have nothing to do with ours. In certain situations, it is very important to wonder whether we are like Job's children. They never shared in any great way in their father's promises in being part of God's plan for that situation (Job overcoming a great trial). Or, we can be like Job who, after great testing, received a ten-fold reward. Either way, we are supposed to, in all circumstances, accept our part in God's plan in fullness of faith and in service to the glory of God.

Our idea of "planning" can also be likened to the farce-like and irreverent movie called *Evan Almighty*. In the movie, the Evan character is trying to live his life with some normalcy while the God character is asking him to be like Noah and to build an ark. Evan complains to God for fouling up his life and his plans, to which the God character responds, chidingly, "YOUR plans?"

We, like children, often don't understand when a wise parent sees the bigger picture and has a better plan. So it is with trusting God for all that we desire and even things that we may not ask for, including a deeper relationship with Him... God sees the bigger picture.

Luke 11:9 (ESV) "*And I tell you, ask, and it will be given to you; seek, and you will find; knock, and it will be opened to you. For everyone who asks receives, and the one who seeks finds, and to the one who knocks it will be opened. What father among you, if his son asks for a fish, will instead of a fish give him a serpent; or if he asks for an egg, will give him a scorpion? If you then, who are evil, know how to give good gifts to your children, how much more will the Heavenly Father give the Holy Spirit to those who ask Him!"*

God can influence the desires of our hearts but, if ever we tend to struggle with God's plans, I think it is when we want to parent and He does not respond to open the womb. I am blessed to be one of the Hannah's who pleaded with God and received according to my wishes, so I am careful when I speak to friends who did not receive that gift. Yet, I must say this much... I believe the Lord is able to give even to a barren womb and, if He does not, I believe it is important for that couple to go forward in the knowledge that He is always able. They do not ever have to question being in His will, if they submit their lives totally to Him. He has them in His hands and He will use the life that is submitted to Him for great things - even if that person has children naturally, adopts, or remains childless - as long as they continue to trust Him for good things.

When my children were young, I sang with them a song I made up for them that was from the Bible verse in Proverbs 16:3 (KJV). We sang, "Commit your works unto the Lord and He will establish your thoughts." In Proverbs 16:9 (ESV) it says, "The heart of man plans his way but the Lord establishes his steps." I wanted my children, whom I knew were planned more by God than by me or my husband, to grow up imbedded with the understanding that God made them and that they owe it to Him to let Him guide all that they do. I wanted them to experience the same fulfillment I had when entrusting my plans to the Lord.

With my sons growing and needing me less and less, I find myself desiring an even deeper intimacy with the Father than I've ever had before. I still remember the day that I first realized I no longer felt the constant tug of my youngest son at my pant legs anymore. Here I am, years later, realizing that I am the one pulling on my Father's pant leg. The experience of parenting, if it has transformed me in no other way, has allowed me to see through a parent's eyes that there is great joy in your child trusting you with everything. This has freed me to come to God with more abandon in my expression of love for Him and awareness that He is always there for me when I am hurting.

Luke 18:16-17 (TLB) *"Then Jesus called the children over to Him and said to the disciples, 'Let the little children come to Me! Never send them away! For the Kingdom of God belongs to men who have hearts as trusting as these little children's. And anyone who doesn't have their kind of faith will never get within the Kingdom's gates.'"*

Isaiah 40:11 (ESV) *"He will tend his flock like a shepherd; He will gather the lambs in His arms; He will carry them in His bosom, and gently lead those that are with young."*

Luke 18:27 (ESV) *"But He said, 'What is impossible with man is possible with God.'"*

Matthew 6:26 (NIV) *"Look at the birds of the air; they do not sow or reap or store away in barns, and yet your Heavenly Father feeds them. Are you not much more valuable than they?"*

Hebrews 11:6 (ESV) *"And without faith it is impossible to please Him, for whoever would draw near to God must believe that He exists and that He rewards those who seek Him."*

## *Prayer*

Dear Heavenly Father,

When fear entangles my soul, and *Light* seems to evade me, I look to the *East* for the *Sun* to rise and bring forth new hope. For You promise, Lord, that Your mercies are new every morning and You are the *Sun* and the *Hope* that rises in the proverbial *East*. Help me, to always look to You; my *Eastern Light*. Help me to never set my eyes on the fleeting fancies of this world that only bring comfort for a moment and, then, are gone. For You never promise me every comfort in this world, but You do promise me that You will be present to strengthen me for endurance and to use my life for Your good purposes when I trust You at all times, through all things. Help me, dear Lord, to stay close to You because it's in that closeness that the things of this world will lose their hold on me. Give me a desire, daily, to worship You, to praise You, and study Your Word. I long to become more like You.

In the name of Jesus, Amen

*Chapter 7*

# His joy was my strength

*I*t was Saturday evening, the twenty-sixth of June 1977. I had dropped off to sleep in my chair in the living room and woke up with a start. Our daughter Patty was at work in a nearby convenience store and we were supposed to pick her up around ten o'clock, when the store closed.

But when I was unexpectedly startled and awakened, I thought, *Patty... who's picking* up *Patty?* I even spoke this aloud to myself. "It's time to pick up Patty!" It was as though an alarm clock had gone off. I felt an urgency to go right away. But, looking at my watch, I saw there was still twenty minutes before the appointed time. So I sat back not realizing I was getting a signal in my spirit alerting me of my daughter's danger. My husband George went at ten o'clock to pick her up.

Patty had completed her freshman year at George Washington University in Washington, DC and was currently working at a nearby Cumberland Farms Convenience Store during her summer break. In 1977, choices were slim for temporary summer employment. I knew she would have preferred something better.

My husband George called later shouting, "Patty has been kidnapped by two men at knife point!"

I was stunned. Could this really be happening? He informed me that a woman waiting in her car for a pizza next door had witnessed what happened. This apparently occurred just minutes before ten. She had alerted the pizza place what had transpired, but they took no action. This convenience store was between the city limits of Boynton Beach and Delray Beach and in a county designated area. The delay in getting the proper authorities to respond to the situation was very frustrating. Valuable time was lost, but this woman was willing to stay at the scene and provide vital information to the deputies and followed up as an eye witness testifying at the trial of the kidnappers as well. May God bless her!

After hanging up the phone, I prayed, "Oh God, if ever I needed You, I need You now." It took me awhile to grasp what was going on. I was truly in shock. I hardly had a chance to tell our son David when the doorbell rang. There stood a boy expecting to have a date with Patty. I think I blurted out, "She's been kidnapped!" He must have thought I was kidding, the way it came out. I still hadn't fully comprehended what had taken place. I usually am the type of person to count to ten before reacting. Since it was Saturday night, I hesitated to call our pastor that late, but when I did, he and his wife came right over to pray and stay with me. They helped me collect my thoughts and make the calls to my family in New York. We sat by the pool, feet dangling in the water, talking and trying to remain calm. When I distinctly felt a "stab" in my heart, I took note of it, looking at my watch. It was a few minutes after one o'clock in the morning. Later, it was determined that 1:00 am was the approximate time of Patty's death.

Later, when George and I were alone, we were watchfully awake in bed, hoping to hear a word from the police and praying all night. We went to church in the morning and sat in the balcony. During the responsive reading, which happened to be Psalm 91, we both sensed, at the same time, the wonderful presence of the Lord. We joined hands, acknowledging a great peace surrounding us. Joy rose up in our hearts. It was hard to explain—a joy and peace that passes understanding.

About six months prior to this, we met with a small group on Monday night at the Methodist Church in Delray Beach for Bible study, prayer and worship. It was our introduction to the Charismatic Renewal. This group, headed by Catherine Marshall, was comprised of other believers that were not necessarily from our church but they had been invited to hold their meetings there. But, this particular Sunday, several from that group were present for a baby dedication. We felt drawn to them and took comfort in their fellowship actually rejoicing in the midst of our crisis at the conclusion of the service.

This presence of God stayed with us and sustained us for many days; first, waiting for Patty's whereabouts, then, through the memorial service in Florida and the trip to New York for the funeral and burial service. God, very much so, arranged for every detail. The July fourth weekend brought my entire family together at our Seneca Lake summer cottage. All of Patty's cousins were there to celebrate her homecoming.

But, I'm getting ahead of myself. My testimony, as well as my husband George's, started back when we experienced the baptism of the Holy Spirit together, only five days prior to Patty's kidnapping. As we studied the Word of God during these Monday nights, it began to take root in us. It was George's idea to attend these meetings and we looked forward to going as the Bible became more real to us. We were already born again and served in the church all our married lives and raised the children in the church as well. But we recognized this as "something more" and we wanted it.

It's amazing how the little bit of God's Word we knew back then was enough to sustain us and enable us to overcome our tragedy. Now that's God's grace! A phrase from a Lutheran liturgy rose up in me on that Tuesday, "The Lord be with you and with your spirit". I muttered that all day long, believing that Patty would be found. It kept me steadfast in my faith. God met me where I was. During this time, the FBI became involved. It was headline news and the psychics wanted in on it too. However, staying focused on God was paramount. When Wednesday came, I was confident that she would be found. I had never turned on the news at twelve o'clock noon before. They broke the news before my pastor or the FBI agent arrived. But how she was discovered is worth noting. At the Lantana Landfill facility, a worker on his lunch break noticed a flock of birds converged in an area apart from the landfill's usual bird activity and he became curious which lead him to where she was.

The previous Monday evening we had attended the prayer meeting where the Lord had spoken a word into George's spirit which he shared with me on our way home.

George told me the Lord spoke into his spirit, "Don't cry. Patty's with Me." It was then that I realized, through the Holy Spirit, that Patty was now with the Lord in Heaven. God had prepared us for the inevitable but finding her was uppermost in our minds. Tuesday had become a day to stand in faith and trust God. The FBI detective arrived shortly after noon on Wednesday to confirm the news about Patty.

When he announced, "We have found your daughter's body," all I could think about was how thankful I was that she was found and declared, "Praise the Lord!"

This was my immediate response. I think he was expecting me to fall apart or something. The look on his face reflected apprehensive relief. The power of God's love, joy and peace had manifested itself so strongly in us that I had no idea the effect it would have on others. The memorial service on Thursday evening seemed like a wedding reception. It comforted us to know Jesus had provided a better place for Patty. That comfort enabled us to bring comfort to our family and others. The gift of joy during this time was so powerful that George and I could not suppress it if we wanted to. It carried us throughout the rest of our lives. Remaining in God's presence brings joy. Whenever I get down, I reflect back to that time when the joy of the Lord was so supernatural that losing our daughter in the prime of her life (with such great potential) would have been devastating had I not been baptized in God's love. The knowledge that Patty is safe in Heaven and established with Jesus for eternity is awesome.

George had a vision of Patty in a blue jumpsuit running through a meadow in Heaven while we were on our way to New York and, later, had a word of knowledge concerning her activity in Heaven as a student of God's Word. I believe that this gift of joy was imparted to us because we first cried out to Him and trusted in Him from the start. He gave us the power to forgive and remain steadfast in that forgiveness. We were able to understand that those men were separate from the evil working in them. Our fight was not against them, but the devil. The press headlined our statement with: **Kidnap Rape Murder!** The article noted that we had also forgiven those men. No one could imagine anything worse happening to a daughter, and yet, we were able to forgive.

She was tall, blond, beautiful and athletic. She ranked third in her high school graduating class and interned her senior year in the Palm Beach County Victim Aid Services and represented Palm Beach County at the National Internship Convention in Washington, DC meeting all the congressmen and recognizing them all by name. She participated in all the Fourth of July Centennial events in Delray Beach in 1976. She was accepted in a special group of thirty students specializing in governmental/ political studies while at George Washington University. She participated in the inauguration of President Jimmy Carter by helping to direct congressmen into their transportation buses. Yes, she was patriotic.

Forgiveness, how did it come so quickly? By the grace of God! It was just a knowing in our spirit to do it. The power of the Holy Spirit was over-riding our minds and it was the natural, or should I say the supernatural, thing to do. We believed what the Bible says about forgiveness and it was very plain in the Lord's Prayer and in Luke 6:37 (ESV) *"Judge not, and you will not be judged; condemn not, and you will not be condemned; forgive, and you will be forgiven."* Had we not chosen this path early on, I believe we would never have been blessed with the comfort and overcoming joy of the Holy Spirit. George and I were in strong agreement about this.

Although Patty's time on earth was cut short, I believe her potential greatness has been extended into the heavenly realm and God gets all the glory and it has been his grace that enabled us to accept it.

George went home to be with the Lord this year and is now together again with Patty. My destiny remains ongoing and the joy of the Lord will be my strength.

Nehemiah 8:10 (ESV) "*... and do not be grieved, for the JOY of the LORD is your strength.*"

## Prayer

Dear Heavenly Father,

I thank You that it is through the constant awareness of Your presence and our intimate conversations that I've been empowered to walk through this nightmare. It is only in the knowing of Your love and forgiveness for me that I have been able to forgive the murderers of my child. Lord, You have taught me to look at others through Your eyes. I know You died on the cross for them as much as You died on the cross for me. Because of my relationship with You, Father, I don't hate these men. I hate the evil that is at work in them. I pray that they will, one day, accept You as their Savior.

I thank You for the time You gave me with Patty. Every moment was a joy. I know she is lighting up Heaven as she lit up our lives here on earth. I thank You for the message of hope that You have given me in the scriptures in the book of Revelation. You have promised a Heaven with no tears and no death. I look forward to that day of celebration when Patty, George, and I will be in Your presence walking on streets of gold. Together, as a family, we will be able to worship You as our King.

Father, I pray for the readers of this book who have lost a child. Heal their hearts and give them hope. May they be able to forgive in order to receive the freedom and peace that comes with every act of forgiveness for those who extend mercy. Let Your words from the cross; "Father, forgive them; they know not what they do" resonate in their hearts. Comfort them where they are. Wrap Your arms tightly around them until they are smothered in Your love. May they look beyond their present trouble with the realization that we are just passing through this earth. May they receive You as their Savior and rest in the assurance of an eternal home with You and their beloved child.

I ask all this in the name of Your Son, Jesus.

*Chapter 8*

# slam dunk for Jesus

*M*y heart leapt for joy when they told me it was a boy; another precious gift from God. Christopher J. Timmons was born on Easter Sunday, April 15, 1979, an answer to my prayer. I remember the first time he had a ball in his hand; seeing his eyes light up with a look of wonder on his face and always bouncing and throwing that ball every chance he got. Basketball was his life. Watching every game on TV, learning all he could about the sport, and playing every chance he had. That is what gave him such joy.

As the years went by, watching him grow playing with his siblings, doing all the things kids do, gave me such loving memories. What a treasured time it was having fun as a family!

At eight years old, he started playing basketball.

I always told him, "When your ready to throw the ball, just do it in Jesus' name. Then, watch what happens!"

He never seemed to forget those words. He wrote them down and then put them on the refrigerator. If you are a mom, you know the refrigerator is the most important place for growing boys. I put Bible verses there for him. It was our secret place for correspondence. He would respond to these verses and stick them in my Bible for me to find later. This always put a smile on my face.

His favorite Bible verse was 1 Peter 3:4 (KJV) *"But let it be the hidden man of the heart, in that which is not corruptible, even the ornament of a meek and quiet spirit, which is in the sight of God a great price."*

Chris had such a caring and a tender heart; yet he was so quiet. His tenderness brought us closer, through the years.

Christopher came home late one afternoon from one of his games at Eastmont Park. I was in the kitchen getting dinner ready, when I heard the door close. I spun around and saw his face. His eyes were cast down and his hands were behind his back.

Hesitantly, the words came out, "How did you do, Chris?"

Then all of a sudden a big smile came across his face.

He shouted with joy and he lifted his hands and said, "I did it Mom, I did it!"

"What did you do, Christopher?"

"I made the final point for our team!"

"How's that, Christopher?"

"Well, JT threw me the ball, I took the shot, and down it went right in the basket. Not only that, Mom, when I threw the ball I said, "IN JESUS' NAME," just like you told me to do; and it worked, just when our team needed it the most."

We both had big grins on our faces and gave each other a big hug.

"Son, I'm so proud of you and happy for the team. But, most of all, for you giving thanks to Jesus. He sees your heart and loves you so very much, honey."

"Thanks, Mom, and thanks for praying for me."

"Anytime, Chris; anytime."

One Sunday, after church, as I was reading our church newsletter, I came upon an article from the men's prayer group. It said that they were sponsoring boys from ages eight to sixteen for the Magic Basketball Camp. I thought to myself... *Wouldn't it be awesome if Chris was selected.* God answered a mother's prayer. They chose Chris!

I still remember the surprised look on his face when I told him, "Christopher, I have some good news for you."

"Okay Mom, let's hear it."

"Well, the church selected you to go to the Magic Basketball Camp this summer."

His eyes opened so wide, with such a surprised look on his face. He let out a loud scream and started laughing and jumping up and down. We both started thanking Jesus.

"Mom, who would do this for me? I know this cost a lot of money for this camp."

"I don't know, sweetie, except God touched someone's heart and you got the blessing. We never know what Jesus is up to, but I do know He loves you. His plan for us is to trust and believe and most of all love Him."

After Christopher found out he was going to the Magic Camp he also found out that one of his best friends he plays basketball with got picked too.

"Mom"

"What is it honey?"

"Ryan got picked for the camp too; we are going to play a one on one together."

"That sounds great."

"I don't know Mom. He's better than me."

"Well, I'll be praying for you. Just throw the ball in Jesus' name. Then, wait to see what Jesus can do."

Summer seemed to take forever to arrive that year for Chris. All he thought about was the Magic Basketball Camp.

When it was time for the camp to begin, I asked Chris, "Are you ready for the big week?"

He answered, "I hope so Mom, and I've practiced every chance I could."

The entire time my son was gone, I prayed that he would have an unforgettable memory there. When I arrived at the church to pick Chris up when he returned, he jumped in the car and gave me a big hug.

"Well, son, I guess you enjoyed the camp."

"Mom, it was one of the best times of my life. You're not going to believe this, but I won the one-on-one with Ryan."

"Why wouldn't I believe it? You know whose got your back."

"Sure do. My Jesus, and that is just what I did. Slam dunked the ball, each time, in Jesus' name, and down it went. He is really there for me, isn't He Mom?"

"Yes, honey, He is." I gave Jesus a big high five and thanked Him for His help.

Chris looked at me and said, "Mom, can I ask you a personal question?"

"What is it son?"

"Did you play basketball in school?'

"Listen son; let me tell you something about your MOM."

"Wait a minute, Mom, aren't you a little short to play basketball?"

"Just because your Mom is short doesn't mean I couldn't run fast or hit the ball off the backboard. You know how it is…. Keeping your eyes on the ball at all times, then, when the time is right, throwing the ball to the backboard and watching it go in. Honey, playing the sport you love and giving it all you can is all you need to do. Be positive. If you learn something from a defeat, it isn't a loss, and you're always a winner."

The Chicago Bulls won the championship that year and they were going to be at Disney World.

"Mom, can we go out to Disney so I can meet the Chicago Bulls?'

"That sounds like fun, so let's do it. Chris, I have an idea."

"What's that, Mom?"

"I'll buy a basketball and when you meet the players, you can get them to sign the ball for you."

"Mom, what a great idea! You're awesome."

"Thanks honey. You're not too bad yourself."

At Disney World, after we got the signatures, we were about ready to leave the park.

Then Chris said, "Look! Over there, Mom, at those people standing in line to see if they can make the shot from the foul line. Can I do that?"

"It's late and we need to get home."

"Please, Mom, please," he retorted.

Knowing how much this meant to my son, I gave in.

"Ok, then that's the last thing we're doing."

Christopher's turn was up and he was the only kid in line and all the adults were cheering him on. I was standing by a tree watching and praying. He missed the first three shots.

Then Jesus took over as I prayed; "Bless my son, God, help him get the shots in Jesus' name."

As I was praying, my hand made the motion to get the ball in the basket. Every time Chris threw the ball, it went in as if Jesus Himself was right there with him. I just kept my eyes closed saying in Jesus' name. He made all seven shots out of ten. Seeing his face, with the biggest smile, made my heart proud and happy. As they handed him his prize winning t-shirt, all the adults clapped their hands. He reached for the t-shirt and held it high over his head walking off with a huge grin on his face.

On the way home he said, "Mom, I made the shots."

"Yes, you did! Your helping Hand was right by you all the way."

"What do you mean, Mom?"

"Well, every time you threw the ball, I said, 'in Jesus' name.'"

"I did too, Mom! Isn't there a Bible verse that says, 'when two or more agree together in My name, there I am with them?'"

"You're on the right path, honey. Jesus will never leave us. We may stray away from Him, but He always finds a way to bring us back to Him."

Christopher was now on his own journey, believing and trusting his own faith in God.

"Mom, would you drive me to the basketball court tonight?"

"OK, after you finish your dinner and homework."

"Will do, dude."

Chris always called me "dude" or some other cute name. When we got to the basketball court, he sat on the bench in hopes that the older guys would ask him to play. He sat there and watched until one of the guys looked over and nodded his head to come on over. Chris flew off the bench with the confidence of David going to fight Goliath. He was so fast off his feet the guys started calling him the "White Mike". On our drive home, not only would I get thanks, but a big high five.

I'd always reply with, "Anytime, son, anytime." He had a grateful and humble heart which made everyone love him.

One day, returning from school, Chris walked into the kitchen and made this announcement.

"Mom?"

"What is it?"

"I need to go to the store and buy Tootsie Roll pops."

"What do you need Tootsie Roll pops for?"

"I'm going to sell them after school, then save the money to buy basketball cards."

"Did you get permission from your teacher to do this?"

"Yes, Miss Clinton said it was fine as long as I did it after school."

My little Christopher became quite the entrepreneur. He just sat back and watched his bank account grow.

One night, while I was sitting in the bleachers watching Chris play in one of his school's basketball games, I heard a man ask, "Who's Number 12?" Who is that kid that is so fast on his feet?"

I turned around with my head held high and replied, "That's my son Christopher Timmons!"

The man said, "Lady, you got some kid there!"

I answered, "Yes I do sir, thank you."

Chris finished the game and, when we were on our way home, I told him about the comment the man had made about how fast he was.

He just turned around and gave me one of his sweet smiles and muttered, "That was nice of him, Mom. We did well, didn't we?"

"You sure did, sweetie."

Being so humble, he never wanted to take the glory; it was all about the team. Not only did basketball bring him joy, but also a sense of purpose.

After high school, Christopher went part-time to a junior college, worked part-time at a furniture store, and even started his own online business selling "Jesus is My Homeboy" t-shirts. Everything seemed to be going well for him. Yet, he was still an extremely quiet person and never talked much. But he always let me know when he was taking the younger kids in the neighborhood to the basketball park.

"Make sure you ask their parents," I would say.

He'd always reply, "Will do, Mom." He always enjoyed showing the kids different moves he learned and giving them advice and encouragement.

Although things seemed to be okay with him, we noticed he was becoming even more withdrawn. We felt he was spending too much time on his computer playing video games. He didn't even want to talk or socialize with his friends like he used to. He decided one day that it was time for him to live on his own and not depend on Mom anymore. The family was supportive and felt he was ready for this responsibility. In the back of my mind, I was still concerned about his quietness and did my best to get him to talk more but he would just smile and say something nice to avoid a conversation. I tried to accept that this is who he was and continued loving him; never dreaming that anything was wrong. After all, although he was quiet, he was always funny and great to be with. Little did I know that this was when my son's life did a total turn around.

While vacationing in New York, I received a shocking phone call that every parent dreads.

I picked up the phone and a deep voice I didn't recognize said, "Are you the mother of Christopher Timmons?"

I could barely answer, "Yes, I am."

The voice introduced himself as Officer Clark with the Seminole County Police Department.

"Is my son okay? Where is he?" I screamed into the phone.

I began to shake all over and started to cry.

"What's going on?" I yelled.

Officer Clark replied, "Your son's alive, Mrs. Timmons. He took a knife and cut himself. We have taken him to Seminole Hospital."

By now, I was a mess with worry, and needed to get home as fast as I could. My friends got me on the first plane home.

I began to ask God, "My sweet Christopher! God, what's going on? Why God why?" The flight home seemed to take a lifetime; all I could do was to ask God the same question over and over, "Why? What did I do wrong?" I prayed, "Be with my precious son now. Let him know You are there with him. My tears won't stop, Lord."

When I got to the hospital and saw Chris, the first thing he said to me was; "Mom?"

"What honey?"

"Will Jesus forgive me?"

By now all I could do was weep, but I held it in for my son and replied, as I gave him a kiss, "Oh Christopher, Jesus forgave us at the cross."

"Mom, will you say the Lord's Prayer with me?"

"Sure son!"

We said the Lord's Prayer together and, by this time, he was falling asleep.

I sat there and thought back on when I was growing up in the church. I would pray to, someday, have a child that is born on a holiday. God granted this request when He gave me Christopher who was born on Easter Sunday. He was such precious gift from God. But now, with these things he was doing to himself, he could die. As the guilt invaded my mind I began to pray, "Why God would you give me this child for this to happen. What can I do Lord to help him? Help me Lord, don't take him from me."

Chris got out of the hospital and then went right into a rehabilitation center. They put him on all sorts of anti-depressive drugs; which made him worse. The rehabilitation center was a two hour drive. My car was only holding up by the grace of God. During the long ride the tears would not stop. A constant prayer was on my lips, "God, Why God, Why?" The rules at the center only allowed visitation for one hour at lunch and dinner and you could bring food in. Therefore, I always took Chris his favorite food.

Seeing and smelling food that he liked, he'd jump up and give me a high five with a hug.

"Thank you mom. You are super!"

We did all we knew to do to help our son. Yet when he got out of the rehabilitation center he attempted suicide again. The third time he succeeded. Now my most precious gift from God has gone home to be with Jesus. Not only is this the hardest thing to write about, but it is also the most difficult memory to live with. Yet, for the healing of my heart to be complete, I must share Chris's story to help others to heal as well. Christopher went to his favorite park where he loved to play basketball and hung himself on a tree. I know, now, how God, the Father, must have felt when He saw His only son hang on a tree. I also know how Mary's heart must have broken when she buried her son.

My final prayer to God for my son Christopher was, "Oh God, help me to release this child that was lent to me back to You. I know he is in Heaven with You and I will spend eternity with him. You hold all my tears in a bottle, Lord. Thank You for the time You gave me with him. I give Christopher back to You, Lord." Psalm 23:6 (KJV) *"Surely goodness and mercy shall follow me all the days of my life and I will dwell in the house of the Lord forever."*

As a mother and a believer, I do not dwell on the dangerous drugs that impacted my son because I know someday these tears will end forever and I will, once again, hold my beloved son in my arms. Christopher believed in Jesus, accepted Him as his Lord, and relied on Him as his Savior. That is all I need to know. 2 Corinthians 5:8 (KJV) *"We are confident that to be absent from the body we are present with the Lord."*

God gave me this Bible verse, Acts 3:6 (KJV) *"Silver and gold I have none, but what I do have I give to thee"*. We didn't have much, but we had the most wonderful mother-son relationship in the world. We owe it all to Jesus.

The day we returned home from Christopher's funeral, his brother John found this song he had written among his things in his room:

# Thank You

### By Christopher Timmons

*If it wasn't for you, I wouldn't be here.*
*Even though you're far away, I kept you near.*
*Writing you this song is the only way I can express,*
*The way I feel towards you.*
*If it wasn't for you,*
*I wouldn't pray.*
*Everything you've done, I haven't forgotten,*
*Those late night dinners you used to make.*
*We never had much, just you and me,*
*But we always had enough to make us happy.*
*All those years you carried on for me,*
*Just a single mother trying to make ends meet.*
*You always made sure I had what I wanted,*
*Never let me go to school unless I had enough.*
*I haven't forgotten about the things you did,*
*That day has come and I thank you Mom.*
*You might laugh at this next line,*
*But I hated that red car.*
*However, when we'd ride together,*
*I felt like a star.*
*My love for you is so true,*
*I can't believe how much I'm missing you.*
*Now what am I supposed to do?*
*Your baby boy is all grown,*

*About to start a life of his own.*
*I learned a lot from you,*
*For all this I say THANK YOU.*
*Always had clothes to wear, food to eat,*
*A roof over my head, sports to play.*
*You gave up so much for me,*
*Can you believe I am finally starting to see?*
*Why couldn't I see what was right in front of me,*
*Every thought I had was about you.*

What the enemy meant for evil, God turned around for good. God always brings life out of a death situation. So is the birth of "Slam Dunk for Jesus". This ministry was started in the name of Christopher Timmons to sponsor youth to attend the Orlando Magic Basketball Camp. While I was grieving for my son, God gave me the gifting to design and create ear rings, key chains, and also boot, cell phone, and purse eye-catching accessories. The proceeds from the sale of this merchandise is being used to support this ministry. This endeavor became known as "One of a Kind Designs: Purseology Decor". I have extended the outreach to support the veterans and the homeless. This has brought me comfort over the years to bring God's healing message to those who I have met as a result of my ministry. I know that this is what Christopher would have wanted me to do with the talent the Lord has given me. He always enjoyed helping those less fortunate.

Slam Dunk Mission Statement: "*This ministry is impacting our youth and young adults through the sport of basketball. This mission will build lasting values though seed planting, as we unite out lives and reach the lost in remembering Christopher Timmons who found Jesus on the basketball court.* IN JESUS' NAME"

## Prayer

Dear Heavenly Father,

I want to tell You I love You with all my heart. I want to thank You for giving me my son, Christopher. He always brought a smile to my face. When I was down, he had a way of making me laugh. When he was gone, I kept wondering if there was something I could have done to change his choice. I felt guilty because I didn't do more. Next came anger, hurt, blame and the loneliness. I felt abandoned when he committed suicide. I never got to say goodbye. What could I do with these feelings and emotions but run to You, my loving Father. There You were, with open arms, just waiting to take my pain and replace it with Your joy. In Isaiah 53:3, it says that You, Jesus, were acquainted with deepest grief. You knew what I was going through, and You watched Your own Son die a death that He didn't deserve. I believe that, one day, Christopher will run up to me, as I enter Heaven, where we will be together for all eternity. You are preparing a home for us there. I wonder if it will have a basketball hoop?

Father, I especially thank You for this creative gift that You have given me to help others. You have used my products that You have helped me design to minister to the people You have brought across my path. Many of them have lost a child and are still hurting. You have blessed me to be used by You to share

Your love, healing and hope with them. I ask You to continue to use me, dear Lord; especially, may this book be a tool to bring comfort and restoration to women.

I ask all this in the name of Your Son, Jesus.

## Chapter 9

# chad sees.... his story

*I* woke up January 16, 1987, and quickly ran to the bathroom where, instead of the normal morning routine, my water broke. Little did I know, that the next time this event took place it wouldn't be so routine. When I arrived at the hospital, they took me right in and fitted me with a blood pressure cuff on one arm and an IV on the other. My doctor arrived soon after I did and stated that I had some time. I hadn't fully dilated.

A couple of hours later, when one of the nurses came in to check on the baby's status, she had trouble finding her heartbeat. At that same moment, the blood pressure machine that had been automatically taking my blood pressure at regular intervals started to beep wildly indicating that my blood pressure was very elevated. I could see, from the look on the nurse's face, that something was very wrong.

Upon deciding to perform an emergency C-section, they wheeled me into the operating room while I heard my doctor yelling urgently in the background in his thick French accent. When he approached me, however, he was very calm and reassuring. Krissie was delivered and appeared to be healthy, at first. The doctors' concerns, at that time, were focused on me since I had lost a large amount of blood due to the elevated blood pressure and had also had an allergic reaction to one of the pain medications. They had to give me other medications, to counteract the allergic reaction, as well as give me a transfusion of two pints of blood.

Due to the seriousness of my condition, I was under heavy sedation for the next two days and barely remember what took place. The only comment I remember was that of two doctors that entered my room to tell me that, after further examination, they had discovered a hole in Krissie's heart. However, they didn't think it would be a serious situation.

I remember one of them saying, "Let's face it. She just won't be a track star." The second visit from the doctors was much different. On that occasion, they said it was more complicated than they originally thought. Krissie would have to undergo a heart catheterization to try to find what the real problem was.

After six days in the hospital, Krissie and I were allowed to go home. She had red hair, blue eyes, and a perfectly shaped head (thanks to the C-section); unfortunately, after the heart catheterization and echocardiogram exams, it was discovered she only had half a heart. The doctors decided to wait it out to see if they could perform a procedure to help her after she got a few months older. I was given one word of advice by doctors after that particular visit: Make sure she doesn't cry. There were occasions when I had to blare the stereo in the car so that she wouldn't cry. A strange technique, perhaps, but it seemed to work. Unfortunately, about two and a half months later, she was struggling to breathe. We rushed her to the emergency room and they flew her to Shands Hospital in Gainesville where she remained until she passed away on June 3, 1987.

I know you are probably wondering by now why the name of this story is ***Chad Sees***. Well, I couldn't talk about Chad and the struggles we went through without first talking about his sister, Krissie.

Fast forward to December 16, 1987…I was one week from my five-month high-risk pregnancy office visit and going to work at my new position at Disney in the insurance department.

I went to use the bathroom and my water unexpectedly broke. One of my coworkers, who I had only known for two days, drove me to the hospital.

When I arrived at the hospital, the nurse met me with a wheelchair and happily said, "It looks like someone is ready to have a baby."

I quickly turned and looked at her and replied, "I'm not even five months pregnant." I saw all the color drain from her face, and she rushed me into a delivery room. There was a frenzy, at that point, with many nurses and other personnel rushing in and out of my room checking on my condition and that of the baby. They said they were going to slow down the delivery and that lasted until the next day when they were no longer able to find a heart rate. While my doctor kept reassuring me that all would be okay, he was being far less optimistic with my mother. He told her that they were going in to get the baby but were expecting it to be stillborn. They took me into the delivery room and had me push only once. He was born with no sound whatsoever. Immediately after he was born, they put Chad in an incubator and intubated him and used a bag to help him breathe.

Once they were able to get him somewhat stable, Dr. Faup stepped out into the waiting room and told my mother, "Zee baby he is alive!", again, in his very-thick French accent.

Right before Chad was born, a doctor, who was working with me before my regular doctor arrived, told me that Chad never would be anything but a lifeless lump with a heartbeat. I never really understood why he said that to me. Maybe it was about my decision to have a C-Section or not. Several years later, I found myself in the same elevator with that doctor who had made that prediction. I was at the hospital taking Chad for a checkup.

I looked up at him, while holding Chad, and said, "Some lifeless lump!"

Chad's statistics were as follows: Weight: 1 pound five ounces, a little over seven inches long, a grade-two, stage-three brain hemorrhage, and a hematoma the size of his back. When Dr. Alexander, the neonatologist, came in to talk to me, he told me that Chad would only have a five percent chance of survival through that first day. You could look back at the year I had (having lost Krissie) and understand the feelings and thoughts I was dealing with at that moment. But for some reason, I found myself assuring the doctors that Chad was going to be fine.

The next day, his lungs collapsed and he had to have a chest tube put in. Again, the doctors thought it didn't look good and that he probably wouldn't survive the second night. As before, I told the doctors that I was sure Chad would make it, even though I didn't know where my confidence was coming from.

Once Chad was stable, I noticed that he wouldn't track my finger or look at me or anything. A test was performed that discovered he had Retrolental Fibroplasia; a fancy term meaning he had detached retinas. Chad was blind.

He came home from the hospital a day before his original due date of April 8, 1988. They say that having a child with a disability or losing a child can end a marriage. When you have both occur, it makes it easy for a marriage to fall apart.

In 1990, I moved to Pennsylvania so that Chad could attend the Overbrook School for the Blind, in Philadelphia. I was very young when I had Chad, and moving to Pennsylvania as a single mother made me grow up very quickly since I had none of my family close. However, I was blessed to have Dave, the man that Chad today knows as "Dad," share those years with me in Philadelphia and become a true father to Chad.

During the first few years, Chad was always a very loving and happy little boy in spite of all the physical and developmental challenges that he faced and his many visits to the hospital at all hours of the day and night. He could also be hard to handle, more than your typical toddler. It would literally take an hour just to get him to go down one flight of stairs or to transition him from one place or activity to another.

There were many years of different therapies: feeding clinics, mobility specialists, and occupational therapists. That was a full-time job for me. It was so difficult to get any kind of respite from caring for Chad that I actually dropped him off at a day care facility in hopes that they wouldn't realize that he was completely blind. That didn't work out very well and didn't last for even a day.

Around the age of five, Chad was diagnosed with Pervasive Developmental Disorder (PDD) which is in the spectrum of autism. His milestones were different from those of other kids in that one of my goals for him was to walk into a McDonald's, order a Happy Meal, and sit down and have dinner with him. That was impossible, partly because of the PDD and his behavior at that point in his life.

He seemed to really like music and joined the choir at The Overbrook School. I can remember a time when he was about two and I had music playing on the stereo. Chad, before he was really walking, pulled himself up to the stereo and changed the channel until he found a Sinatra station. He knew what kind of music he liked, even at that young age. Music was used in his therapy and it always seemed to calm him. Even when he was still in his incubator, the hospital personnel would play music he could hear within his bed. Taking part in the chorus seemed to be a great motivator to help Chad improve his behavior. He started to acquire a fondness for Gospel music and it eventually led him to look for and listen to Christian radio stations that played Christian music and programs as he got older.

One day, when Chad was about eight or nine, I had to go to his school to attend an IEP (Individual Education Plan) with his teachers.

On the way home from school, Chad piped up and asked me, "Mom, what color are you?" And I said to myself, "Oh, boy. Here we go." I said to Chad, "I am white." To which Chad replied, "Oh, you are the same color as Nicki." (Nicki was his best friend from school)

I continued telling Chad, "No, honey. Nicki is black."

Chad answered right back, "No, mom. Nicki is in the white group in our class. I am in the black group and Brett is in the green group." At that moment, I realized that Chad would never judge anyone by his or her appearance. He sees people for who they are and doesn't care about their color or what they look like.

There came a time when Dave and I parted ways, although he continued being a very big part of Chad's life. At the age of 13, we moved back to Florida so Chad could attend the Florida School for the Deaf and the Blind. This was a big change for us because it was a boarding school, and the bus would pick him up on Sunday and drop him off on Friday. I remember that the first day I dropped him off at the bus stop, I followed it all the way to St. Augustine and cried all the way home.

Chad needed to be around kids with similar struggles in order to help him with his social skills while learning life skills that I probably would have taught him had he remained living at home with me. He thrived at school, while meeting several friends with whom he is still close. He loved his teachers and especially his dorm parents who served as his replacement parents while he was away from me.

Around this time, as he continued listening to Christian programs and Gospel music on the radio, and he would always ask me questions about it. Chad was learning about God from a radio station and not from his mother. God was pulling him close, even at the age of 13.

I know that, although I was not really following God during my ordeal with Krissie and during the times with Chad and me, God was certainly following and looking out for both of us.

During his yearly visits to Philadelphia to visit Dave, Chad would fly there and back by himself.

On one of those occasions, when his grandmother went to pick him up at the airport, she asked him, "Chad, how did you like flying so high in the air?"

Chad was puzzled because, all the time he flew back and forth, he never realized that the airplane was actually leaving the ground.

In 2006, Chad graduated from FSDB, although he continued to attend until the age of twenty-two as a

Continuing Education student. After his graduation, FSDB focused on his independent living skills and prepared him to attend the Conklin Center for Multi-handicapped Blind, in Daytona Beach.

In December of 2007, I met a Christian man who would eventually become my husband and introduced me to our church and reintroduce me to God. I remember when my husband proposed to me... Chad interjected, "Good luck with that!" Chad doesn't understand sarcasm so he literally meant what he said.

During his time at Conklin Center, from age twenty-two to age twenty-three, Chad was taught many basic life skills, such as, grocery shopping, personal hygiene, money management, mobility, and other important tasks. Toward the end of his stay there, he was trained for and given a job at a local Papa John's restaurant folding pizza boxes, once a week. He loved to work and excelled at it, so much so that, upon completing the program and returning home to Orlando, he was given that same job in one of the busiest Papa John's in the Southeast. He continues working there three days a week, to this day.

Chad has many friends, grandmothers, grandfathers, aunts, uncles, cousins and even a step-sister who love him very much and their love, influence, and support have helped mold Chad into the fine young man that he is today. He has even been mentioned, by name, by our Pastor, in a Sunday message, as an example of joy in spite of adversity. Chad continuously ministers to others and speaks about God to those he encounters on the bus, at work, or anywhere else he finds himself.

John 9:1 (NKJV) *"Now as Jesus passed by, He saw a man who was blind from birth. And His disciples asked Him saying, "Rabbi, who sinned, this man or his parents that he was born blind?" Jesus answered, "Neither this man nor his parents sinned, but that the works of God should be revealed in him. I must work the works of Him who sent Me while it is day. The night is coming when no one can work. As long as I am in the world, I am the Light of the World."*

## Prayer

Dear Heavenly Father,

Thank You for Chad. There are so many things we can learn from him. He does not look at people with his eyes, but he sees them through his heart. I reflect on the scripture, John 20:29 (NIV) where Jesus says: *"… Because you have seen Me, you have believed; blessed are those who have not seen and yet believe"*. Chad accepts the Word of God with "blind" faith and trust. Help me to live according to 2 Corinthians 4:18 (NIV) *"So we fix our eyes not on what is seen, but on what is unseen. For what is seen is temporary, but what is unseen is eternal"*. I do not want to look at things through the eyes of this world, but through the eyes of the Spirit. I know, in seeing things this way, I will be able to totally trust You and live in Your perfect peace knowing that You are in complete control. Although we live in a world where there is constant struggles, tragedy, and heartbreak I thank You that we are never alone. Let me never forget that this isn't our last stop. Give me a hunger for Heaven and for eternal things. I desire a deeper relationship with You. Help me to see as Chad sees.

In the name of Jesus, Amen

## God's Boxes of Love

I have in my hand two boxes,
Which God gave me to hold.
He said, "Put all your sorrows in the black,
And all your joys in the gold."
I heeded His words, and in the two boxes,
Both my joys and sorrow I store.
But though the gold became heavier each day,
the black was as light as before.
With curiosity, I opened the black,
I wanted to find out why.
And I saw, in the base of the box, a hole,
Which my sorrows had fallen out by.
I showed the hole to God, and mused aloud,
"I wonder where my sorrows could be."
He smiled a gentle smile at me,
"My child, they're here with Me.
I asked, "God, why give me the boxes,
Why the gold, and the black with the hole?"
"My child, the gold is for you to count your blessings,
the black is for you to let go."
—Author unknown

*Chapter 10*

# afterword

The compassionate women who shared their heart-rending stories in this compilation want to first honor and glory to God for allowing them to contribute to this book. Their prayer is that the readers will:

- experience the God that they did
- be inspired to draw close to God
- be assured that they are never alone in their suffering
- lay their burdens at the feet of Jesus
- receive the way of forgiving love
- know that the Holy Spirit will comfort them and that Jesus will heal them

Where was God in your worst and darkest hour? He was right where He was when His Son was crucified and died that horrific death on the cross. He was right there! Not only is He a Father who cares but He is a Father who understands how deeply you hurt. He knows what it is to cry. At His friend Lazarus' grave, Jesus cried. How do you handle it when your dream is interrupted by tragedy? Let the cross be your symbol of hope in the midst of your most harrowing circumstances. It gives meaning to the cruelest of all human suffering. God sent His one, and only, Son to the cross so that we might receive the gift of salvation. Therefore, we should be able to realize how God can use suffering to bring about His purposes. He used the sacrifice of His Son to bring about the greatest purpose for our lives and the lives of our children - - to live with Him, forever, in eternity. He is able to use our suffering to accomplish His purpose. It was love that sent His Son to the cross for us and He continues to love us with that everlasting love.

John 3:16 (KJV) *"For God so loved the world, that He gave his only begotten Son, that whosoever believeth in Him should not perish, but have eternal life."*

Psalm 34:18 (ESV) *"The Lord is near to the brokenhearted and saves the crushed in spirit."*

Matthew 11:28-30 (NLT) *Then Jesus said, "Come to Me, all of you who are weary and carry heavy burdens, and I will give you rest. Take My yoke upon you. Let me teach you, because I am humble and gentle, and you will find rest for your souls. For My yoke fits perfectly, and the burden I give you is light."*

Psalm 139:1-12 (ESV) *"Oh Lord, You have searched me and known me! You know when I sit down and when I rise up; You discern my thoughts from afar. You search out my path and my lying down and are acquainted with all my ways. Even before a word is on my tongue, behold, Oh Lord, You know it altogether. You hem me in, behind and before, and lay Your hand upon me. Such knowledge is too wonderful for me; it is high; I cannot attain it. Where shall I go from Your Spirit? Or where shall I flee from Your presence? If I make my bed in Sheol, You are there! If I take the wings of the morning and dwell in the uttermost parts of the sea, even there Your hand shall lead me, and Your right hand shall hold me. If I say, 'Surely the darkness shall cover me, and the light about me be night,' even the darkness is not dark to You; and the night is bright as the day, for darkness is light with You."*

Psalm 22:10 (ISV) *"I was dependent on You from birth; from my mother's womb You have been my God."*

John 14:1-3 (KJV) *"Let not your hearts be troubled. Ye believe in God; believe also in Me. In My Father's house are many mansions; if it were not so, I would have told you. I go to prepare a place for you. And if I go and prepare a place for you, I will come again, and receive you unto Myself; that where I am, there ye may be also."*

Romans 8:18 (ESV) *"For I consider that the sufferings of this present time are not worth comprising with the glory that is to be revealed to us."*

Revelation 21:4 (ESV) *"He will wipe away every tear from their eyes, and death shall be no more, neither shall there be mourning, nor crying, nor pain anymore, for the former things have passed away."*

Before you close this book, I want to give you the opportunity to know the God whose love the women in these chapters testify to. You can give your heart to Jesus today, with the certainty that that He will welcome you. Make sure to allow Him to be Lord of your life, and He promises that He will prepare a beautiful place for you in Heaven. Please, pray this simple prayer aloud:

*Dear Jesus,*

*I am sorry for my sins. I believe You are the Son of God. I believe that You suffered and died on the cross in my place and that You rose again. You did this so that I could live with You for all eternity. You are in heaven waiting for me. Thank You for loving me so much. Come into my heart, change me, and help me to live for You. I accept You as the Lord and Savior of my life.*

If you prayed that prayer today or would like to share how this book has been a blessing to you, I would love to hear from you. Contact me at: **Dejah05@gmail.com**

# epilogue

I believe that the Holy Spirit's purpose for inspiring me to write this book is to bring a message of hope and healing to anyone who has lost a child, nearly lost a child, or who has a *special* child. Even though we do not have answers to questions we might have regarding our children, we can be certain that they will be answered when we see Him face to face. As believers, we have the assurance, by faith, of an eternal home (Heaven) that God has prepared for us because He loves us. There, we will be clothed with garments of praise and with robes of righteousness and glory. We, also, have the assurance that the children who have had an early departure from this earth are in God's presence fulfilling their purpose in heaven. The moment a child departs from this earth, they are immediately in the arms of their loving Father.

2 Corinthians 5:8 (KJV) "*We are confident, I say, and willing rather to be absent from the body, and to be present with the Lord.*"

9 781630 477301